Plugged In!

A Teacher's Handbook for Using Total Quality Tools
to Help Kids Conquer the Curriculum

CAROLYN WICKS, JANET PEREGOY, and JO WHEELER

Illustrations by Penny King

© 2001 Carolyn Wicks, Janet Peregoy, and Jo Wheeler

All Rights Reserved. No part of this publication (with the exception of perforated pull-out pages designed for customer copy privileges) may be reproduced, stored in a retrieval system, or transmitted, in any form or by means electronic, mechanical, photocopying, recording, or otherwise, except for the inclusion of brief quotations in a review, without prior permission in writing from the publishers.

ISBN 0-9715564-0-7

ClassAction
Coast to Coast Connection
P.O. Box 3040
New Bern, NC 28564-3040

Printed in the United States of America.

FOREWORD

Foreword

Acknowledgments

We used these tools as we worked through the plan, do, check, act cycle to pull this book together for you. We know this stuff works! There have been some bang-ups and hang-ups along the way, but mostly bright places and boom-bands playing, too! We love working together!

We couldn't have done it without help from some very special folks.

Heartfelt thanks to:

- Our families for their love, encouragement, and support.
- Lisa for her optimism, professionalism, good cheer, and her ability to move mountains.
- Penny for her artistic genius and her ability to be dexterous and deft.
- Teachers from across the country who have contributed to our examples.
- Craven County Schools for bringing us together.

Honor and appreciation to:

- Myron Tribus, Ph.D., for the knowledge, wisdom, and character he has contributed to the field of education.

Throughout this book we refer to *Future Force—Kids That Want To, Can, and Do!*
by McClanahan and Wicks. If you don't already have a copy, get one.

PACT Publishing
3233 Grand Avenue, Ste. N-112
Chino Hills, CA 91709
1-800-858-0579

We also integrate powerful snippets from *Oh, the Places You'll Go!* by Dr. Suess.
Be sure to add this delightful and thought-provoking treasure to your library.

Random House: New York, 1990

For additional copies of
Plugged In—Using Quality Tools to Conquer the Curriculum,
use the order form in the back or contact:

ClassAction
Coast to Coast Connections
P.O. Box 3040
New Bern, NC 28564
1-800-705-6176

TABLE OF CONTENTS

Introduction 1
   Chapter Overviews 6

Chapter 1 ... Fishbone Diagram 17
   Why Use a Fishbone Diagram? 17
      Health Science 19
      Writing 21
      Social Studies 22
      Math 24
      Science 28
      Assessment 30
      Real World 34
      Curriculum Ideas from A to Z 38

Chapter 2 ... Lotus Diagram 43
   Why Use a Lotus Diagram 43
      How Do I Use a Lotus Diagram? 45
      Literature 45
      Math 50
      Science 51
      Writing 52
      Social Studies 56
      Real World 59
      Curriculum Ideas from A to Z 62

Table of Contents

Chapter 3 . . . Affinity Diagram 67
   Why Use an Affinity Diagram? 67
      Culture, Foreign Language, Foreign Literature 69
      Reading 72
      Science 75
      The Arts 76
      Real World 78
      Assessment 82
      Curriculum Ideas from A to Z 84

Chapter 4 . . . Force Field Analysis 89
   Why Use a Force Field Analysis? 89
      Math 91
      Poetry 95
      Social Studies, History, Civilization 96
      Health Science 100
      Environmental Science 102
      Public Speaking 104
      Assessment 106
      Curriculum Ideas from A to Z 108

Chapter 5 . . . Flowchart Diagram..113
Why Use a Flowchart Diagram?..113
- Math...116
- Science..119
- Social Studies...122
- Safety...124
- Literature...126
- Classroom Management...130
- Curriculum Ideas from A to Z...132

Chapter 6 . . . Bone Diagram..137
Why Use a Bone Diagram?..137
- How Do I Use a Bone Diagram?...139
- Writing..142
- Social Studies, Civics, and Economics..144
- Science..146
- The Spiraling Curriculum...148
- Literature...150
- Health Science...152
- Classroom Democracy..154
- Parent Conferences...156
- Real World...158
- Curriculum Ideas from A to Z...160

Table of Contents

Summary 165
   A Few Final Words to Help You Get on Your Way 165

For Your Information 173
   Power Sources 175
   Bibliography and Suggested Readings 176
   Quality Tools Pull-Out Pages 182
      Tool Summary Page . . . .
      Fishbone Diagram (1) . . . .
      Fishbone Diagram (2) . . . .
      Lotus Diagram (1) . . . .
      Lotus Diagram (2) . . . .
      Force Field Analysis . . . .
      Flowchart Symbols . . . .
      Bone Diagram . . . .
   Order Forms for Additional Copies . . . .

A WORD TO YOU BEFORE YOU BEGIN...

...from Carolyn, to Help Ground the Connection!

Before you get started and on your way, we thought you might enjoy knowing who we are, how the three of us came together, and how our work began...

For me, this is not only a way to provide you with a historical perspective, but also a way for me to honor two women, Janet and Jo, whom I have learned to respect, trust, and enjoy tremendously. Let me give you just a wee bit of background...

In January of 1996, I was asked to come back to Craven County Schools to conduct another set of interactive workshops to help teachers implement Total Quality tools in the classroom. I had already learned to have great respect for the Craven County quality efforts—efforts made in earnest, efforts initiated and implemented with the shirt-sleeves of key leadership rolled up for action, efforts nurtured and sustained with vision, knowledge, and sophistication, boosted by a willingness and determination to make things happen. (Yes, it was a delight to work in such a system!)

Anyway, during one of the first "repeat" trips back, I found myself among a new batch of teachers who craved support and evidence that "this stuff" could really work in their neck of the woods. I pondered. I thought. I stewed. Then I consulted with Bill Rivenbark, who was then the associate superintendent, a man with a solid understanding of what the principles, philosophy, and strategies of Total Quality Management could bring to the educational environment—and specifically what this action-oriented philosophy could bring to the classroom.

When I told Bill that this new batch of classroom recruits could sure use some "hard-core proof" that this stuff really does work in a classroom full of kids along with a solid statement from leadership embracing this vision, he smiled and said, "Carolyn, I think you ought to visit two of our teachers. They're doing it, Carolyn. They really are. I'd like to see what you think. One of these ladies, Janet Peregoy, is a high school math teacher who was in your first round of training. The other, Jo Wheeler, is a kindergarten teacher who just picked up a copy of *Future Force* and figured it out for herself. Both of these ladies are dynamite, and their classrooms hum with Total Quality."

Well, I had visited other classrooms across the country and had always enjoyed seeing how teachers at different grade levels took the tools to kids of all ages. I had always experienced great respect for those teachers who were willing to put themselves on the line and try. So, I was anxious to go take a peek. I was not ready for what I was about to experience. I was not ready to be knocked off my feet in awe!

First I went to Janet's high school math class. When I walked in (a total surprise to Janet and her students), every student was actively engaged. Different tables of kids were busy

A Word to You Before You Begin...

using various quality tools in a variety of ways. These kids had the language down, the principles in place, and were doing it! It was a kick in the pants! When Janet and I engaged in conversation, these kids didn't skip a beat . . . they were totally self-contained and absorbed in their "on task" conversations. The room felt more like a high-functioning, professional work place than a class in action.

I left feeling wowed and ready to go visit a kindergarten classroom, thinking I'd best gear down my expectations to embrace a room full of 5-year-olds. I could hear the chatter before I even opened the door, but I didn't have a clue as to what I was in for! I was immediately greeted by a tiny little guy with Down syndrome wearing a MacDonald's hat. This little guy let me know that I was his customer and that he was going to give me quality service. He actually used these words! I was tickled pink. Then my eyes swept the room—flow charts, run charts, check sheets, pareto diagrams, interrelationship diagrams, plus/deltas, and action plans were everywhere. The room was buzzing with little bitty kids talking quality and walking the talk! I was surprised when a little girl asked me why I was crying—I didn't realize that tears were streaming down my cheeks.

My vision was alive in these classrooms . . . beyond my expectations.

From those first moments in Janet's and Jo's classrooms through shared presentations at Quality Conferences across the country, our work and our friendship has continued to grow into the stuff dreams are made of—the stuff only visions of excellence can bring about. We have all traveled different roads on our quality journey, each of us continuing to learn. Each of us knowing that pooling our experience, talent, and enthusiasm for this quality stuff catalyzes synergy at its best.

So, know that when you move through the pages, you are being invited into a world that energizes and engages and inspires the three of us . . . a world that we believe will take you off to great places.

Good luck and have fun!

INTRODUCTION

Introduction

QUALITY PRINCIPLES

Customer Focus

People-Centered

Process Focus

Systemic Thinking

Long-Term Thinking

Scientific and Statistical Thinking

Getting Ready to Plug In . . . Getting Grounded!

Teachers are not screaming, "I want to learn everything there is to know about Total Quality!" Teachers are screaming "Help me cover the overcrowded curriculum. Help me and my students survive and conquer *high-stakes* testing."

So rest assured, the purpose of this book is not to teach Total Quality per se. Our purpose is not to teach the quality story—the history, philosophy, or principles. However, our work is grounded in Total Quality. We believe that the principles and methods of Total Quality are the ticket for *covering* and *uncovering* the curriculum, the ticket for conquering high-stakes testing. We believe that the principles, processes, and techniques of Total Quality are the foundation for creating a learning environment that encourages kids to become the thinkers and doers who can and will confront real world problems—girded with the values, knowledge, and skills they need to be effective, innovative, and successful. We believe that the principles and methods of Total Quality are the foundation for launching kids that want to, can, and will lead us into the future with confidence, integrity, and a spirit of "Let's do it!"

So, while we do believe that it is important for both you and your students to be grounded in quality, we're not going to cover this . . . we're going to provide you with the challenge of uncovering this groundbreaking information yourself. Along the way

---

ISSUE BIN

- Teachers are screaming
- Overcrowded curriculum
- High-stakes testing

DEFINITIONS

Cover:
To place something on, over, or in front of as to conceal; to provide an alibi or subterfuge; to coat or sprinkle.

Uncover:
To reveal; to make clear; to discover.

Now wouldn't you rather uncover the curriculum than cover it?

Think about it!

Introduction

and throughout the book, you will be confronted with challenge boxes, thought ticklers, clues, references, and resources that will lead you to discover and re-discover the quality story so that you and your students can integrate the philosophy and principles necessary to learn, understand, and implement these processes in such a way that they maintain their power and do not simply become a grab bag of tricks.

First off, before tackling the curriculum, you will want to create a learning environment that encourages your students to share ownership and assume accountability. Remember the Ground Rules provided in *Future Force* (pp. 15-17)? They're powerful in creating a synergistic learning environment, yes? Well, here are a few more ground rules to add to your list. Hopefully they will take you even one step further in helping your students create a productive, win-win environment in which everybody learns, everybody participates.

- No judgment, no blame.
- The problem is the problem. The person is not the problem.
- Problems are unsuccessful attempts to resolve difficulties.
- Change happens all the time. Change is inevitable.
- Only small changes are necessary to provoke a larger change.
- Terror-Joy! (*Sometimes those changes we are most afraid of, are those which are most powerful and will bring us much delight.*)

FYI

Did you know that Thomas Edison had 1200 unsuccessful attempts before he invented the light bulb?

When interviewed by the press, he was asked, "How did it feel to fail 1200 times?"

Edison replied, "I didn't fail. I invented the light bulb. It was a 1200 step process."

Think about it!

After grounding the class with these shared values and ways to work together, it's time to look at your curriculum and explore the stated objectives in order to create a vision of what success would look like for your class, to determine your class goals and expectations—the mission of your time together. Don't be afraid to share mandated state or district goals and objectives for your grade or course. Remember: the curriculum is not yours alone. The curriculum is both yours and your student's. The curriculum provides the framework for everything you are going to do, the purpose of your learning experience.

In the following chapters we are going to provide you with vivid examples of how teachers and students have used quality tools and processes to confront and conquer the curriculum. We will provide you with examples of how teachers and students have applied these tools to plan, learn, assess the learning process, and assess the results.

> **CHALLENGE**
>
> - Who is W. Edwards Deming?
> - What are the fourteen points?
> - Who are your primary customers?
> - What does it mean to be people-centered?
> - What is a process?
> - What is systemic thinking?
> - What is long-term thinking?
> - What is scientific and statistical thinking???

FISHBONE DIAGRAM ... CHAPTER 1

You're gonna get hooked, don't ya know! When you throw out your line and fish for facts, tidbits, or creative ideas, you will lure the kids into a learning experience that not only initiates systemic thinking, but also explores cause and effect relationships in the content and process of your curriculum.

Using a Fishbone to Teach Curriculum

We've provided you with an overview of the fishbone diagram and how it can help you uncover your curriculum.

Health Science

In this example you'll see how this clever fish discovers the ins, outs, highs and lows of a healthy heart. You can't beat that!

Writing

Narrative, descriptive, fact or fiction—this fish adapts to its environment and helps express any point of view effectively, efficiently, and thoroughly to boot (fishing boot, that is!).

Social Studies

We've mentioned Thomas Edison. How about Ben Franklin?

Math

A rat in the house might eat the ice cream, but math is math is math from counting pennies to calculating probabilities.

Science

Labeling causes of a polluted environment not only explores cause and effect relationships, but becomes a method for taking notes, studying, and reviewing for quizzes, finals, and state testing.

Assessment

From formative assessment to summative assessment and right into the portfolio—get your attention? Hope so!

Real World

Field trips, authentic assessment, team activities and performance tasks: mere frills? Of course not! When you see how kids have used the fishbone to plan a trip or sheet-rock a house, you'll quickly see how the fishbone quickly translates into an action plan, shared responsibility, accountability, and pride in workmanship.

Curriculum Ideas from A to Z

At the end of each chapter we provide tons of ideas that you can browse through to tickle your own thoughts and get you to start plugging in right away. In this chapter we've provided you with examples from language arts to guidance to vocational education.

Introduction

LOTUS DIAGRAM . . . CHAPTER 2

Just as a lotus flower unfolds, learning unfolds. The lotus is virtually a learning window that encourages individuals to become "system thinkers."

Using a Lotus Diagram to Teach Curriculum

Just to get you started, we've provided a process that will help you and your students plug this tool into your curriculum.

Math

Want to get a new angle on teaching geometric shapes to kids of all ages? Try a lotus diagram to help kids organize, analyze, synthesize.

Science

What do you know about the classes of vertebrates? You've got a backbone. Don't be afraid to probe a little and find out what your kids already know about a topic!

Writing

I don't know what to write! No problem—the lotus diagram can cure "blank paper panic." Try it, you'll like it!

Social Studies

Don't be afraid to "branch out" when your class is studying about our branches of government. Use a lotus diagram to help kids generate and organize information—tackle the curriculum!

Real World

Get rid of those first-day jitters! Use a lotus to start planning for the first day of school. A solid step to ensure that everything will run smoothly!

Curriculum Ideas from A to Z

Lots of ideas.

AFFINITY DIAGRAM . . . CHAPTER 3

Uncovering the curriculum is a complex undertaking . . . and the affinity diagram is a robust process just right for the job! This technique taps into the right brain and the wrong brain. Just kidding—this tool taps into right-brain and left-brain thinking.

Foreign Language or Foreign Literature!

In this example, kids brainstorm, organize, categorize, and analyze—while touring France in a whole new way!

Reading

From fairy tales and fables to novels and poetry, the affinity diagram can help kids explore literature in a way they'll never forget.

Science

There's nothing the matter with this great science example! Check it out!

The Arts

So what makes a vocal (or dramatic, instrumental, and even athletic) performance truly world class? Kids can use the affinity to establish criteria for excellence while also investigating the notes, pitch, and strikes.

Real World

Math and the real world meet in this dynamic real-world problem-solving experience. From brainstorming, to categorizing, to an action plan, these kids make their math curriculum come to life.

Assessment

But what do they really know and how do you know they know? How do they know if they don't know that they don't know? That is the question. Why wait until the big test to find out? With an affinity diagram, you can determine what kids know and don't know, and can help fill in the gaps.

Curriculum Ideas from A to Z

From left to right and beyond . . . !

Introduction

FORCE FIELD ANALYSIS . . . CHAPTER 4

Force field analysis is a great exploratory and decision-making tool, encouraging great thinkers to think even more deeply, uncover more ground, and probe even further into the depths of critical and analytical reasoning to conquer the curriculum.

Math

Gotta have wheels! Teenage kids dream of owning that first car—a force field puts them at the wheel when making that decision. Smaller kids have smaller decisions, but the force field helps them, too!

Poetry

Move on down the road with the force field as your guide—it's quite a trip!

Social Studies

From Native Americans adapting to their environments, to immigrants coming to America, to elementary kids exploring democracy—the force field encourages higher level thinking.

Health Science

We've got the skinny on fad diets—take a look!

Environmental Science

Singing in the rain . . . forest.

Public Speaking

The brain is a wonderful thing. It starts working immediately when you are born and never stops until the moment you are asked to speak in public!

Assessment

Take me to your leader—could the leader be a kid? In a student-led conference, you bet!

Curriculum Ideas from A to Z

Take a gander.

FLOWCHART DIAGRAM . . . CHAPTER 5

Flowcharts can map out or sequence the stages of a project, the steps of a problem, the phases of any story, situation, or event . . . and the power is not just that the flowchart does this so clearly and efficiently, but rather that it transforms these events, phases, and stages into processes—introducing and reinforcing process thinking, one of the basic tenets of Total Quality.

Math

Let's start things on a positive note—or is it negative? How can kids remember all those rules for operations with positive and negative numbers? The flowchart can help!

Science

We want to plant an idea in your mind—for starters, how to use flowcharts for science experiments!

Group Activities With Math and Science

It's in the bag! What's in the bag? Candy of course! In this "sweet" example, see how the flowchart helps groups work together and solve problems.

Social Studies

How do those bills flow through Congress? What happens after they're passed? Use a flowchart to make it more clear.

Safety

Electrify (not electrocute!) your class when you plug in to a safety flowchart!

Literature

Analyze this! Ever wonder how an author developed the story line in a piece of literature? Get out your magnifying glass and a flowchart and start looking for clues.

Classroom Management

Do your kids ever ask you "What are we going to do today?" Why don't you ask them instead?

Curriculum Ideas from A to Z

Flow with these possibilities.

Introduction

BONE DIAGRAM . . . CHAPTER 6

To effectively uncover the curriculum, you and your students will have to identify and articulate the current state, envision the desired future state, and analyze the gap between here and there . . . and then of course identify goals to achieve, tasks to reach your goals, the driving forces that will help you get there, and the restraining forces that may impede progress. The bone diagram is a tool that helps students to visualize and document this strategic planning process from start to finish!

Using a Bone Diagram to Teach Curriculum

We've "dug up" the bone diagram process for you, and here it is!

Writing

Bone up on writing! This elementary example is something you can sink your teeth into!

Social Studies, Civics, and Economics

"Taxation without representation!" But was that the whole story?

Science

Six degrees of separation (or Kevin Bacon, take your pick).

The Spiraling Curriculum

Where do we go next? How does what we're learning this year prepare us for what we'll learn next year?

Literature

Sometimes by the end of a story or novel a character has changed a lot! What drives the change?

Health Science

Here's to your health!

Social Studies

Who's really in charge? In this classroom example, cleanup is everyone's responsibility.

Parent Conferences

Chew on this new idea—a bone diagram to

guide the parent conference and help parents and kids team together to create action plans for improvement.

Real World

Making decisions based on data and using the data to improve—how a bone diagram made it all happen!

Curriculum Ideas from A to Z

Browse, browse, browse.

Introduction

Okay, now you have a hint about what's coming up. As you move from tool to tool and from example to example, bring your kids and your curriculum along for the ride (in your mind, that is). Then, after pondering the possibilities, start working with your students to cover and uncover your curriculum in ways that engage young minds to take the challenge—to take ownership of their learning, to take pride in their workmanship.

Get going!

CHAPTER ONE

FISHBONE DIAGRAM

You get a line and I'll get a pole, Honey . . .
  You get a line and I'll get a pole, Babe . . .
    You get a line and I'll get a pole . . .
      And I'll meet you down at the learning hole . . . !

Why Use a Fishbone Diagram to Uncover My Curriculum?

You were first introduced to the fishbone in *Future Force* (pp. 81-84). So, as many of you know, you and your students can use this tool to approach content in virtually any subject area and at every grade level. In the following pages we are going to take you through a series of "live" examples created in classrooms across the country by teachers and students just like you. Some are using "quality tools" for the very first time, some are well into the quality journey, and others are not involved in a quality initiative in any way, but are using these methods just because it makes good sense from a learning perspective. In this chapter you will move through content examples that represent core curriculum from kindergarten through 12th grade. These examples will provide you with visual guidance to help you take the fishbone and plug it into specific curriculum content and process. As you move through the pages, you will move from

Chapter One

> ### KEY CONCEPTS
>
> ***A Fishbone to Teach My Curriculum?***
>
> Yep! And, it's as easy as pie.
>
> After reviewing the purpose, goals, and objectives of your curriculum, introduce the fishbone as a tool that will help you:
>
> - Uncover information.
> - Discover cause and effect relationships.
> - Organize, categorize, and document your work.
> - Assess understanding.
>
> ### TIP
>
> *Tired of lecturing and preparing lesson plans? Would you like to move from lesson planning to shared learning planning?*
>
> Use the fishbone with your students to:
>
> - Align learning plans and activities that provide clear instructional focus.
> - Assess and document student learning.
> - Create portfolios.
>
> *Would your students benefit from active involvement?*

beginning steps that display basic content, to examples that illustrate planning and improving learning processes, to examples that demonstrate the powerful way in which the fishbone engages students in ongoing assessment.

As you move through sample fishbones created by first graders, sixth graders, or seniors in high school, you will see how these kids have used this tool not only to graphically organize and categorize content, but also to synthesize and analyze information. This hands-on process and visual display of information not only helps students to "anchor down" key learning, but more importantly, creates a learning experience that leads to more sophisticated thinking, encouraging kids to embrace complexity—moving from the concrete to more abstract reasoning and problem solving.

Plugging Fishbones Into Health Science

> ... *a healthy process with scientific rigor!*

The kids who worked on this fishbone first generated basic ideas to reflect categories known to cause a healthy heart—from family history to lifestyle. After initial brainstorming (*Future Force*, pp. 45-48), they continued to flesh out more and more details to expand the information and reflect clearer understanding.

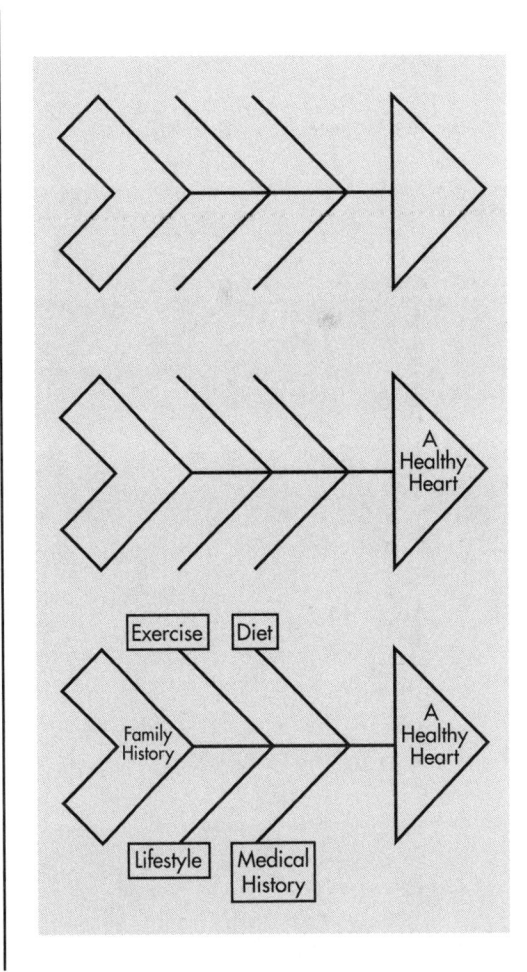

Chapter One

NOTES

CHALLENGE

1. What is the scientific method?

2. What is the PDCA cycle?

3. How does the fishbone tie in to the PDCA?

4. In which phase of the PDCA cycle can you use the fishbone to initiate a quality process?

5. What are the current national standards for science?

Want to know these answers? Check with the "Power Sources" in the back of the book!

How Would a Fishbone Plug Into Writing?

A fishbone is an effective tool for organizing and improving writing at all grade levels. The sophistication, categorization, and detail will vary not only with grade level, but also with purpose and mode—explanatory, point of view, research, or creative. This fish adapts to its environment!

Sample: Elementary

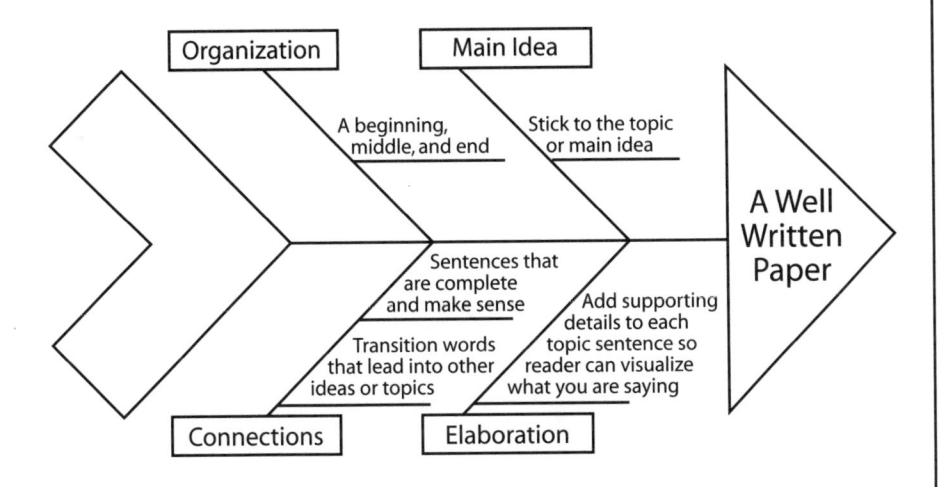

TIP

Using a particular mode of writing in your class?

Use a fishbone to analyze and organize narrative, clarification, point of view, descriptive, or thesis writing, breaking each mode into "chunks" for better understanding!

Fishbone diagram:
- Organization: A beginning, middle, and end
- Main Idea: Stick to the topic or main idea
- Connections: Sentences that are complete and make sense; Transition words that lead into other ideas or topics
- Elaboration: Add supporting details to each topic sentence so reader can visualize what you are saying
- Result: A Well Written Paper

Chapter One

Them bones, them bones, them fishbones . . .

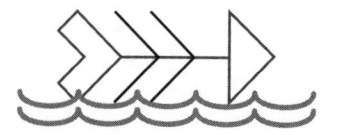

TIP

- There's no limit to the number of bones you can use. Add a bone here, add a bone there, or consider adding a tail!

- In the tail of this fish, students could include information about the times in which Franklin lived.

How About Social Studies?

Sample: Middle School

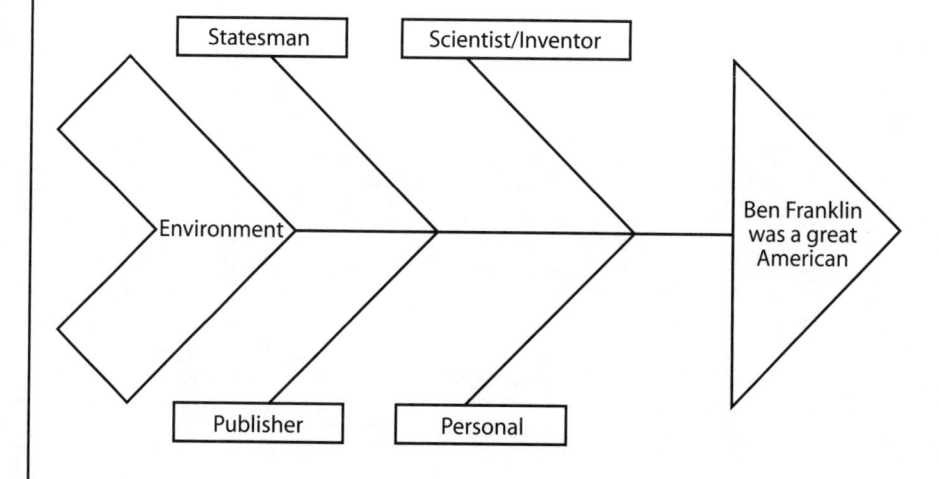

Statesman • Scientist/Inventor • Environment • Publisher • Personal → Ben Franklin was a great American

NOTES

Chapter One

> **TIP**
>
> *Assessment?*
>
> - Why not have students use a fish bone to assess their understanding of money? Put an amount in the head, label the bones, and have them write and illustrate the correct amounts.
>
> - How about having middle or high school kids use a fishbone to assess their understanding of quadrilaterals, equations, or other mathematical concepts?
>
> *What an effective portfolio product!*

Math–Plugged Into Pennies?

Count on it!
 Or divide, multiply, calculate probabilities.
  Yes, the fishbone can be used in math!

Sample: Elementary

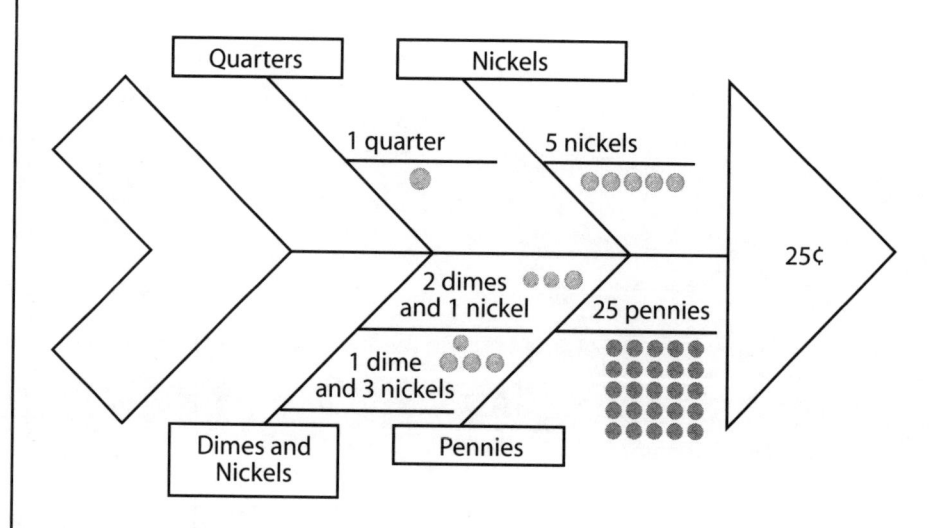

```
        Quarters        Nickels
          1 quarter    5 nickels
             ●         ● ● ● ● ●
                                          25¢
          2 dimes  ● ● ●
          and 1 nickel    25 pennies
          1 dime  ● ● ●
          and 3 nickels
       Dimes and        Pennies
       Nickels
```

As Ben Franklin said,
"*A penny saved is a penny earned!*"

Go Figure!

Yes, you can use this with higher level math. Check out the following examples!

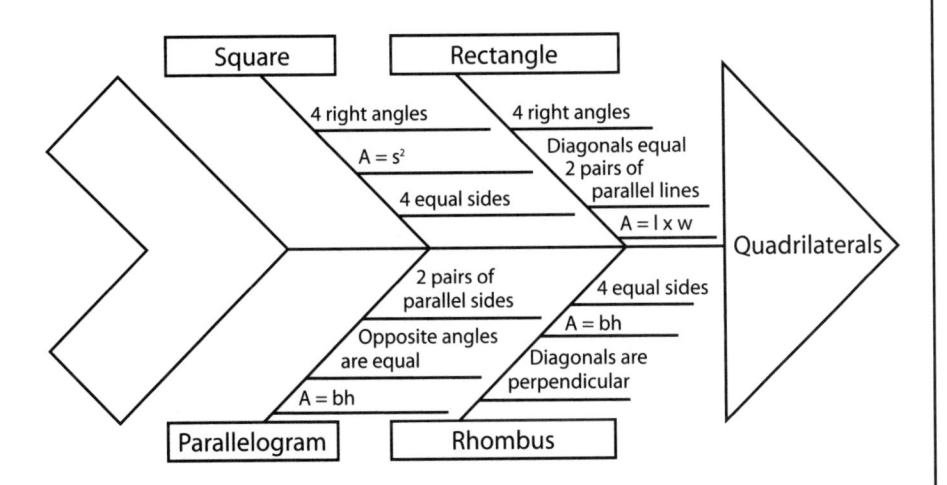

Square: 4 right angles; $A = s^2$; 4 equal sides

Rectangle: 4 right angles; Diagonals equal; 2 pairs of parallel lines; $A = l \times w$

Parallelogram: 2 pairs of parallel sides; Opposite angles are equal; $A = bh$

Rhombus: 4 equal sides; $A = bh$; Diagonals are perpendicular

→ Quadrilaterals

SO HOW DO CONIC SECTIONS PLAY OUT IN REAL LIFE?

An elliptical surface has special characteristics. In an elliptical room, any sound emitted from one of the two foci (plural of focus) is concentrated at the other.

Next time you're in Washington, D.C., be sure to visit the Capitol Building. There is a large elliptical chamber with the location of the foci clearly marked on the floor.

Want to have a little fun with your friends? Have them stand on one focus, while you quickly move to the other and whisper, "I'm over here!" No matter how many people are standing between you and your friends, they will hear you as if you are standing right beside them and whispering in their ear.

Long before there was electronic amplification, the properties of the conic sections were used to enhance sound! They still are. Pay attention to the acoustics in an outdoor amphitheater.

Real life is filled with learning opportunities and examples of practical applications that demonstrate how principles and theories of learning—from math to science to reading and grammar—play out simply in some cases to make life easier, or sometimes play out in ways that astound our minds . . . historical monuments, scientific feats, great literature, and wonders galore.

Live to learn, learn to live!

Fishbone

TIP

A fishbone is a great way to:

- Organize and introduce complexities of higher math.
- Prepare for an upcoming test or quiz.

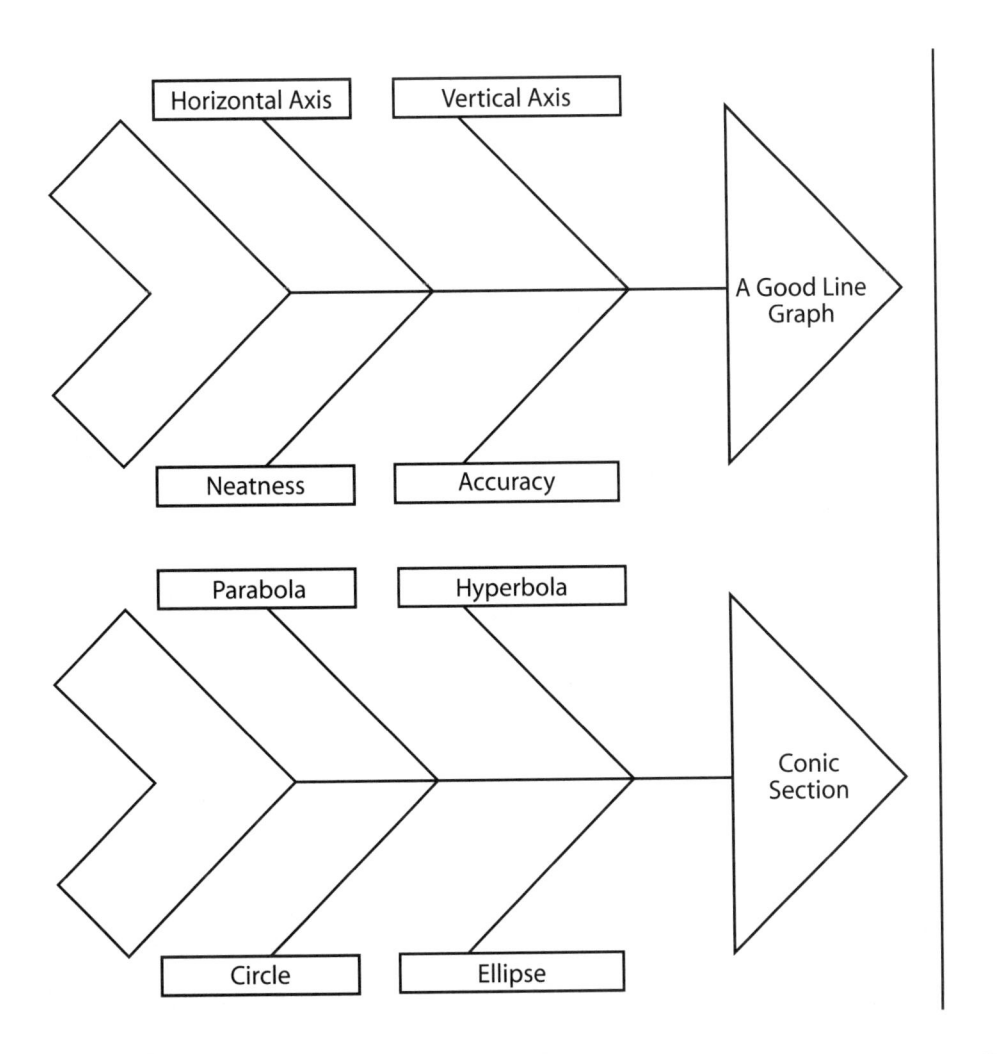

Fishbone 1: A Good Line Graph
- Horizontal Axis
- Vertical Axis
- Neatness
- Accuracy

Fishbone 2: Conic Section
- Parabola
- Hyperbola
- Circle
- Ellipse

27

Down to a Science!

Instead of assigning a chapter and the questions at the end, why not use the scientific method and begin with a question? This teacher tried it and it worked. She began with the question, "What are the causes of a polluted environment?" After labeling four bones and the tail, she assigned the kids the fishbone as a method to take chapter and lecture notes. Individual fishbones of each student contributed to team fishbones, and then to a class fishbone. As the information was gathered and the fishbones grew, understanding grew as well—both for individuals and for the group.

Can you imagine a more effective learning process? How about the student-made documentation as a study guide to prepare for quizzes, final exams, and state testing?

Fishbone

> **TIP**
>
> - Kids love to use this tool as a format for taking notes on a chapter.
>
> - If teams or individuals are doing fishbones to be compiled later into one larger, more comprehensive fishbone, the class can agree in advance on how to label the bones.

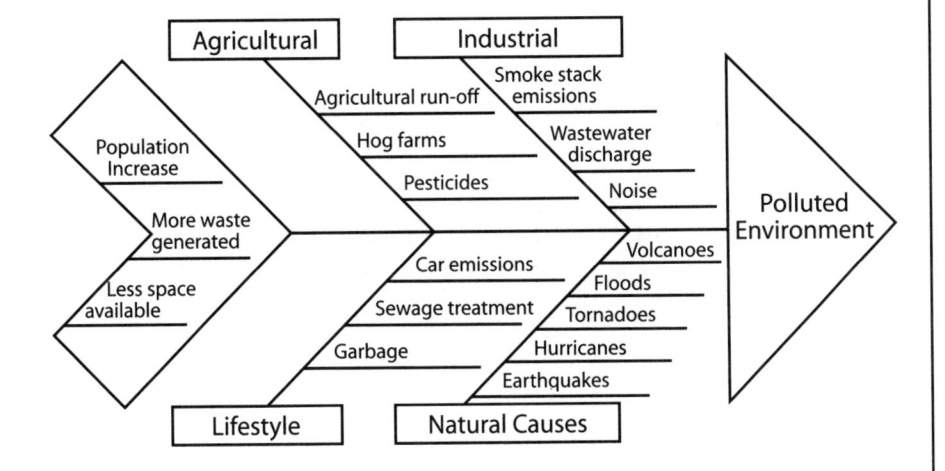

Agricultural
- Agricultural run-off
- Hog farms
- Pesticides

Industrial
- Smoke stack emissions
- Wastewater discharge
- Noise

Lifestyle
- Population Increase
- More waste generated
- Less space available
- Car emissions
- Sewage treatment
- Garbage

Natural Causes
- Volcanoes
- Floods
- Tornadoes
- Hurricanes
- Earthquakes

→ **Polluted Environment**

Chapter One

> **TIP**
>
> **Key Assessment Questions**
>
> *Formative Assessment*
>
> - What processes have been used?
> - What progress has been made?
> - What problems have been encountered?
> - What resources are needed to succeed?
> - Are new strategies needed?
>
> *Summative Assessment*
>
> - What was planned?
> - What was accomplished?

How Do I Use a Fishbone for Assessment?

A powerful part of the learning process is assessment. No! We are not talking about the test at the end of the chapter or the final exam. We are talking about ongoing assessment that is integrated into every phase of the learning process. We are talking about ongoing assessment in which the student is actively involved as the primary player.

In the following examples, the teacher first provided the students with a fishbone complete with the effect written in the head of the fish and with contributing causes identified on each bone. She asked the students to fill in the bones with the appropriate information per category.

Fishbone

Each student used the "bare bones" illustrated below to trigger, guide, and capture their thoughts. Yes, the thinking begins...

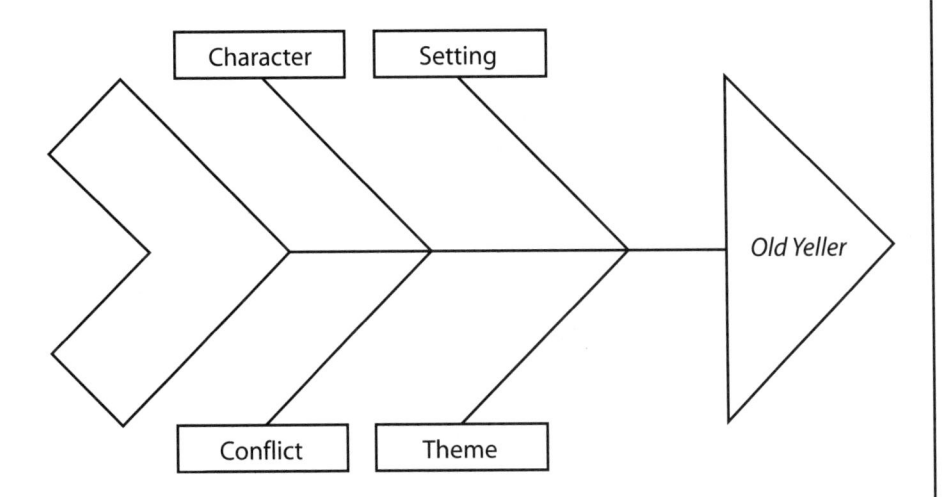

```
      Character    Setting
         |            |
   >>――――+――――+―――――+―――――< Old Yeller >
         |            |
       Conflict     Theme
```

> **TIP**
>
> *Portfolio Production*
>
> - Portfolios are not a dumping ground for all student work!
>
> - Items for the portfolio should be chosen that clearly demonstrate the student's level of understanding.
>
> - Portfolios can and should be updated regularly to reflect most current level of mastery.
>
> - Portfolios can be used as a foundation resource for a parent conference led by the student.
>
> - The "assessment" fishbone diagram is an effective portfolio document!

Chapter One

Surprise! Surprise! She was pleased with the visible display of their work because she was quickly able to identify areas of misunderstanding and opportunities to flesh out needed detail. Review the "first attempt" fishbone.

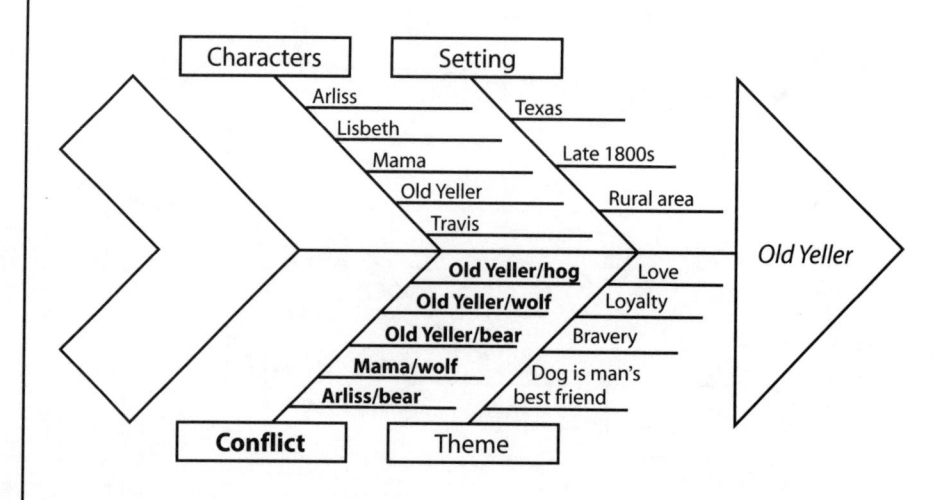

Characters: Arliss, Lisbeth, Mama, Old Yeller, Travis

Setting: Texas, Late 1800s, Rural area

Conflict: Old Yeller/hog, Old Yeller/wolf, Old Yeller/bear, Mama/wolf, Arliss/bear

Theme: Love, Loyalty, Bravery, Dog is man's best friend

Old Yeller

Can you see the opportunities for increased learning? First, this student can flesh out more details to provide a richer understanding of how integral setting is to the plot, theme, and characterization in this story. Second, this student can develop a second fishbone to rethink and expand his understanding of conflict. Check out this teacher's guidance as evidenced in the new and improved "Conflict" fishbone below and the fleshed-out "Setting" bone in the tip box on the right.

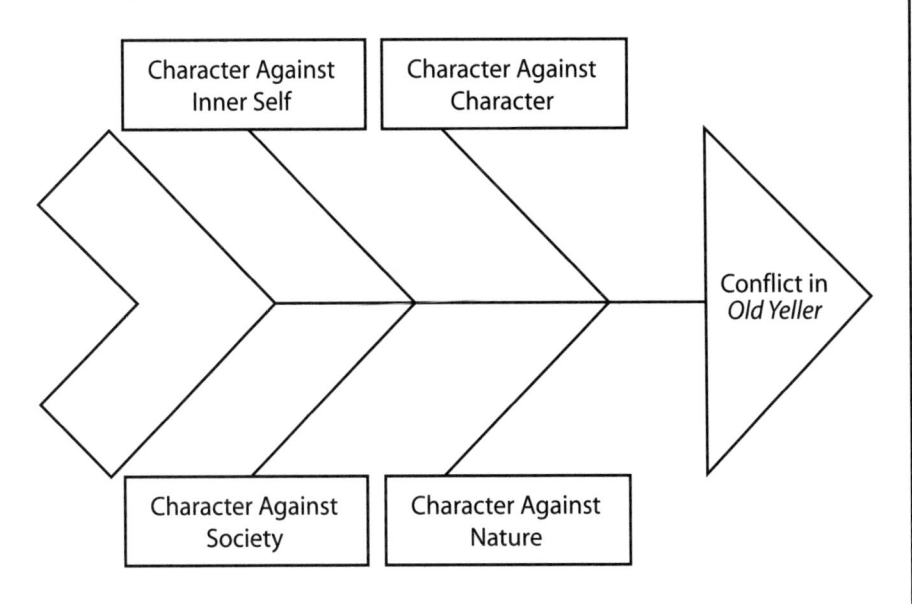

Conflict in *Old Yeller* fishbone:
- Character Against Inner Self
- Character Against Character
- Character Against Society
- Character Against Nature

***Looks like a higher learning opportunity to us!
What do you think?***

> **TIP**
>
> Simple settings can be deceivingly complex! The simplicity of the family farm in *Old Yeller* conveys the challenging, yet rewarding lifestyle of the early settlers. And, the fishbone is a deceivingly simple tool that captures just such complexity!!!
>
> **Setting**
> - Texas
> - Late 1800s
> - Rural area
> - Area first being settled
> - Medical help not easily accessed
> - Remote
> - Neighboring farms provide support
> - No nearby towns

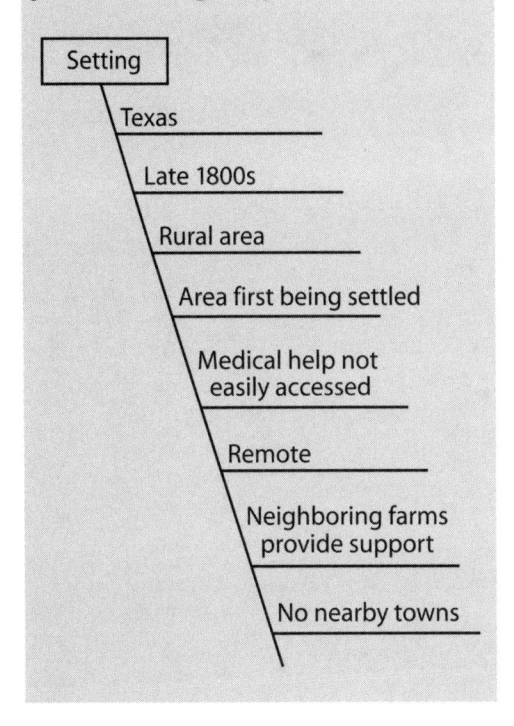

Chapter One

TIP

- Students are stakeholders in the class.

- Create an environment with shared responsibility and shared ownership.

- Quality tools provide kids with the resources and skills to plan, problem-solve, and continuously improve classroom processes.

- The fishbone encourages students to view each activity or event as parts of a system—enabling them to identify cause and effect relationships.

Plugging Into the Real World

Because of the pressure of "high stakes" testing, we are too often tempted to view field trips, authentic assessment, team activities, or performance tasks as unnecessary frills because "we have to teach the curriculum and get the kids ready for the test." No!

What we overlook is that these activities do indeed teach the curriculum—bringing it to life, making it more meaningful, and encouraging the students to connect the significance to the real world.

Just as important, when kids take an active role in planning these events, they also acquire real-world problem-solving skills.

Fishbone

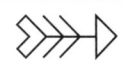

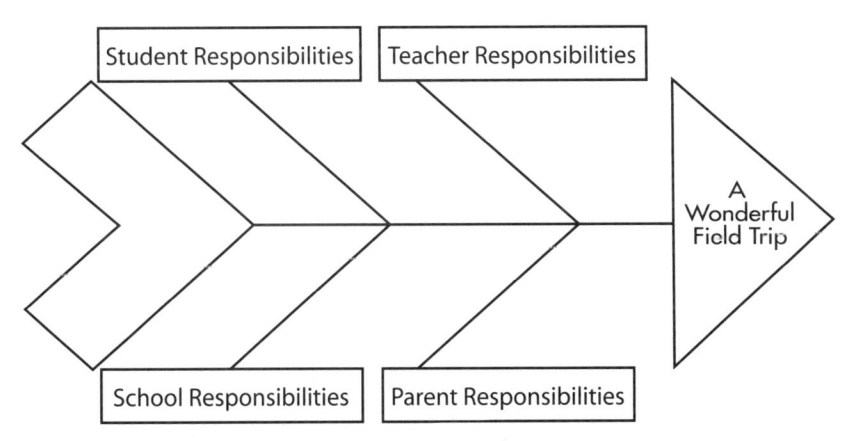

Fishbone Diagram 1

Categories: Student Responsibilities, Teacher Responsibilities, School Responsibilities, Parent Responsibilities → A Wonderful Field Trip

Kids can use this fishbone to create an action plan!

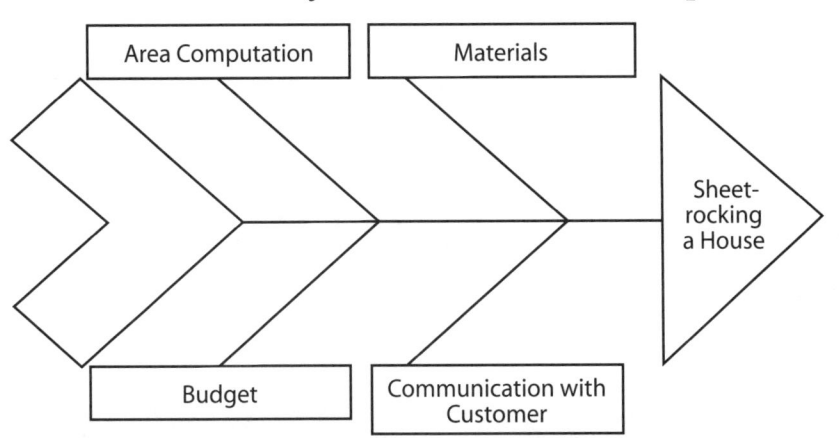

Fishbone Diagram 2

Categories: Area Computation, Materials, Budget, Communication with Customer → Sheet-rocking a House

Think continuous improvement and quality performance!

TIP

Is sheet-rocking a familiar concept to you?

Certainly not to all of the students who tackled this project in high school geometry!

The fishbone not only helped these kids to embrace the reality of a "sheet-rocker" or dry wall contractor, but more importantly launched these kids into higher level learning and the problem-solving process.

REMEMBER THIS EXAMPLE!

Not only are you going to learn more than you ever imagined you'd learn about sheet-rocking in this book designed to help you plug quality tools into the curriculum, but also you will see through this 'rocking' example how students have used various tools in tandem to provide an effective, efficient—and intriguing—learning experience that has moved them beyond the classroom and into the real world. Cool, huh?

Chapter One

A FISH IS A FISH IS A FISH ...

Your fishbone may look different!

Your fishbone may look different. Fish come in many shapes and sizes. Stands to reason, so do fishbones!

Mullet Over...!!!

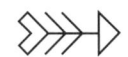

Fishbones Galore!

You have moved through many examples, know the process, and are ready to get started. Remember: there is no one right way. Be creative and have fun!

Think about the purpose, objectives, and goals of your curriculum. What are some ways you can work with your kids to "uncover" this information for your kids? Shared knowledge leads to shared ownership, shared responsibility—shared accountability.

"You have brains in your head and feet in your shoes . . . you can move in any direction you choose."

We've provided a variety of curriculum ideas on the following pages to give you a "head" start!

TIP

- Do try this . . . at home, in the classroom, in school-wide meetings . . . to introduce a topic, plan a project, or review for the test!

- Before you take this into your classroom, you might find it helpful to try one on your own and get the feel of the fish.

- Don't worry, be happy! If you get stuck, the kids can help you get unstuck. Work together!

- Get hooked!

Chapter One

CURRICULUM IDEAS FROM A TO Z

LANGUAGE ARTS

What will cause us to...

- Write a quality research paper?
- Reduce the number of grammar errors in our papers?
- Correctly capitalize the months of the year?
- Use correct punctuation when someone is speaking?
- Recognize the characteristics of a piece of nonfiction?
- Make an informed judgment about a television product?

Other "Causes"...

- What caused the resolution at the end of the story?
- What causes the differences between nonfiction and fiction?
- What would cause an author to illustrate a point in an effective manner?
- What caused the character to behave that way?

HEALTH & P.E.

What would cause...

- Us not to use tobacco products?
- Good sportsmanship during a game?

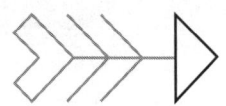

MATH

What will cause us to...

- Regroup (or) rename in subtraction correctly?
- Make sure our work is accurate?
- Add 3-digit numbers correctly?
- Find the multiple of 124?
- Find the equivalent fraction for 75?
- Have a good homework paper?
- Have a well-solved equation?

GUIDANCE

What would cause...

- A good self-concept?
- Us to trust others?
- Us to feel embarrassed?
- Your family to escape from your house safely during a fire?

TECHNOLOGICAL & VOCATIONAL

What would cause...

- A fantastic class multimedia story which includes student narration?
- Us to use technology in the community?
- An excellent meal?
- A good house plan?
- A well-made pillow?

CURRICULUM IDEAS FROM A TO Z

SCIENCE

What causes . . .

- Something to float or sink?
- The sun's changes in position?
- Soil to retain water?
- Us to be able to predict air quality?
- Biological hazards?
- An ecosystem to be able to support life?
- Stream erosion?
- The electrical charging of objects?
- The Doppler Effect?
- Extinction of a species?
- An excellent lab report?

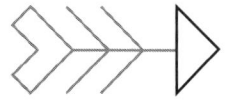

SOCIAL STUDIES

What causes or caused . . .

- People to break rules and laws in neighborhoods?
- Us to be good citizens?
- The need for taxes?
- Government services to change over time?
- The people of the Western Hemisphere to adapt to the physical environment?
- The people of the former Soviet Union to modify their environment?
- The early European settlements in North America?
- Constitutions to grant and limit the authority of public officials and government agencies?
- The colonies to declare independence?
- Failure of the League of Nations?

MUSIC/ART/DRAMA/DANCE

- What caused us to determine this music was from India?
- What would cause appropriate audience behavior for this style of music?
- What causes a good vocal performance?
- What will cause us to appreciate the characteristics and merits of the artwork?
- What causes us to use art materials and tools in a safe and responsible manner?
- What causes good "backstage" behavior?
- What causes the unique characteristics of a drama script?
- What causes the choreographic process when planning a dance?

Chapter One

NOTES

Fishbone

NOTES

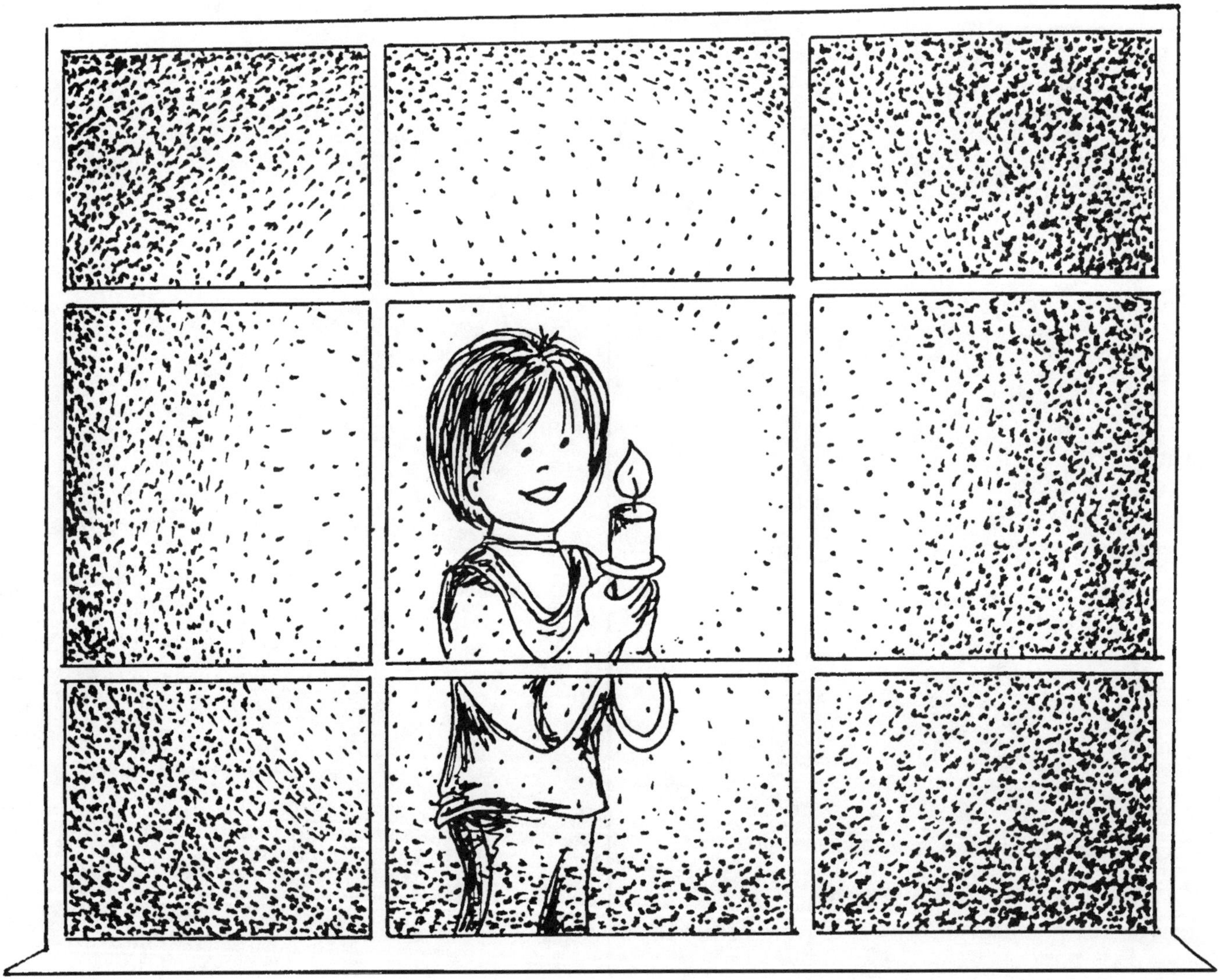

CHAPTER TWO

LOTUS DIAGRAM

" . . . You'll come to a place where the streets are not marked. Some windows are lighted, but mostly they're dark . . ."

Why Use a Lotus Diagram to Uncover My Curriculum?

Yes, yet another tool can be used to approach content and process in any and all subject areas and at every grade level. The lotus is virtually a learning window that encourages individuals to become "system thinkers," recognizing that interrelated parts weave together to make up the whole. As your kids use this tool to confront curriculum content and process, they will not only identify and visually display each part leading to the whole, but will also construct meaning that generates a greater level of understanding and appreciation as they grasp the depth of complexity.

Just as a lotus flower unfolds, learning unfolds. Even as you focus your attention on specific curriculum content and goals geared for a specific age or grade level, the lotus diagram will encourage you and your kids to anticipate and reflect on the ever spiraling learning process. Just as letters lead to words to writing to reading—from basic letter recognition to sophisticated

Chapter Two

> **TIP**
>
> *Want to link learning, critical thinking, shared responsibility, and accountability directly to the curriculum? Of course you do!*
>
> The lotus diagram helps you and your students:
>
> - Identify components of a broad topic.
> - Organize components for further analysis.
> - Prioritize ideas.
> - Design a plan for problem solving.
> - Create a mental model for their thinking.
> - Visually display work for future use.
> - Retrieve information and make critical learning connections.
>
> *and . . .*
>
> Encourages and enables the kids to become the workers in the classroom!

narrative, poetry, drama . . . to complex and rigorous scientific research—so does counting 1, 2, 3 lead to adding and subtracting to algebraic equations and logarithms—or as basic shapes in early elementary lead to basic quadrilaterals in late elementary to quadrilateral formulas in middle school to complex geometry and eventually to trigonometry! Yes, learning spirals from the seeds planted in early childhood to bloom into sophisticated and complex learning.

The beauty of this tool is in its simplicity—the grandeur in its complexity.

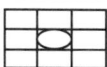

How Do I Use a Lotus to Uncover the Curriculum?

Process

1. Introduce the topic, identifying purpose, goals, and desired outcomes. With your class, discuss how this topic fits into the big picture—this particular course or grade, other course and grade requirements . . . the real world.

2. Introduce the lotus diagram as a tool that identifies, breaks down, and organizes the components of a broad topic—working towards a visual display that demonstrates how interrelated parts construct the whole.

3. Begin with a drawing like this:

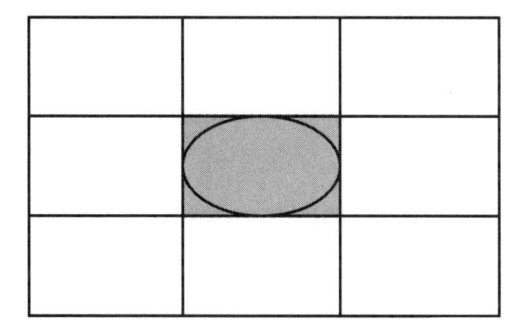

So What's the Difference Between the Fishbone and Lotus?

Well, obviously one looks like a skeleton of a fish and the other a window with panes or a flower in bloom. But, beyond the appearance, their purpose does indeed differ.

Yes, you can use either tool to generate, categorize, and organize ideas, but with the fishbone, remember you are attempting to explore cause and effect relationships.

When using the lotus, you aren't freewheeling like you do with brainstorming because you do indeed start with a central idea and expand outward. From the central idea, you then unfold related categories.

Chapter Two

> **TIP**
>
> Be sure your kids understand they are not limited to just the corner boxes! Their great ideas can fill any and all of the boxes that surround the center box.

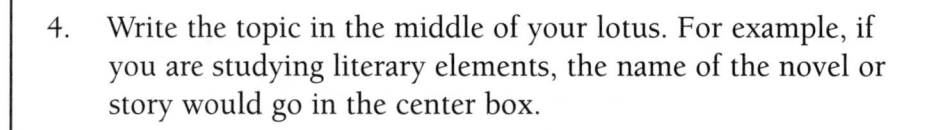

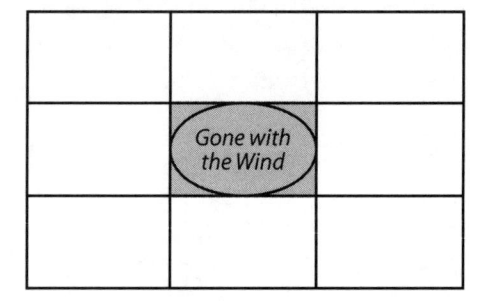

4. Write the topic in the middle of your lotus. For example, if you are studying literary elements, the name of the novel or story would go in the center box.

	Gone with the Wind	

5. As you identify the literary elements or smaller components that you want to analyze, write them in the surrounding boxes.

Setting		Main Characters
	Gone with the Wind	
Resolution		Conflict

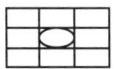

6. Next, take one of the surrounding box components and begin a new box. Continue the process as stated in steps 3, 4, and 5. We've chosen the literary element "setting," and have identified words or phrases that give clues about the setting in *Gone with the Wind*.

Atlanta	Civil War	Deep South
Confederacy	Setting	Plantation
Yankees & Rebels	1860s	Slaves

Chapter Two

7. Now, do the same for each of the other components of your topic. Your diagram will expand or "unfold" to look like this:

Atlanta	Civil War	Deep South
Confederacy	*Setting*	Plantation
Yankees & Rebels	1860s	Slaves

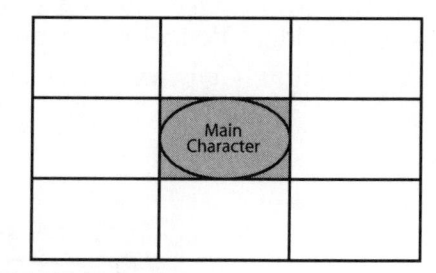

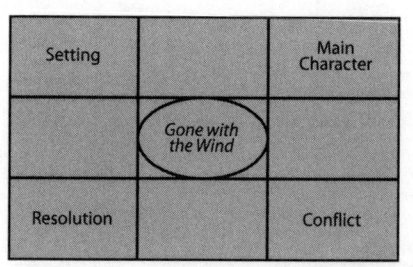

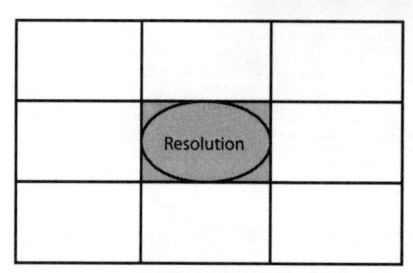

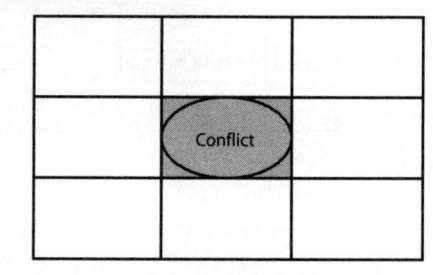

	Main Character	

Setting		Main Character
	Gone with the Wind	
Resolution		Conflict

	Resolution	

	Conflict	

48

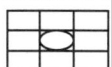

8. Nope, not done yet. The process continues! Any and all of these boxes can become the center concept of a new lotus.

Note: Notice that the boxes are arranged around the center box much like petals around the center of a flower. Imagine the depths to explore if you were to examine the center of the flower—the pistil, stamen, and anthers! Yes the fun continues, the learning goes on and on and on . . .

Rich Soil	Mansions	Tara
Potatoes	Plantation	Peach Trees
Cotton	Mint Juleps	Magnolias

Chapter Two

> **TIP**
>
> *Learning math and building team skills in one fell swoop? You bet!*
>
> This clever teacher had the kids form teams to attack each of the major concepts: rectangle, square, parallelogram, and trapezoid. As each team became "shape experts," they shared their knowledge, contributing to the collective learning experience of the class.
>
> *Sounds like a higher learning experience to us.*
> *What do you think?*

How Would a Lotus Diagram Plug Into Math?

Many kids struggle with broad math concepts and have difficulty breaking those concepts down into smaller parts. A lotus diagram will help them to organize and plan their thinking—which of course initiates effective problem solving.

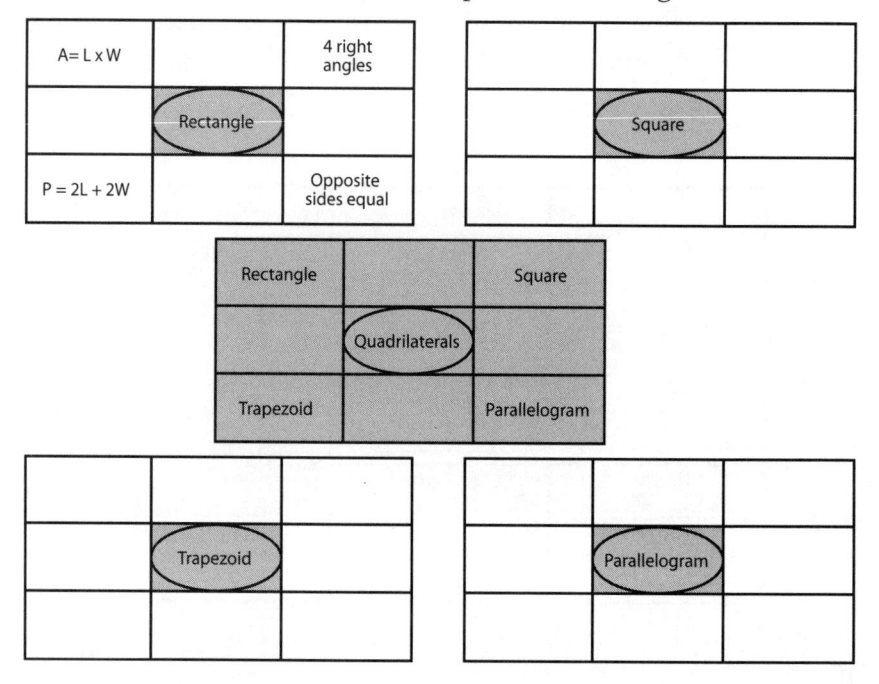

A = L x W		4 right angles
	Rectangle	
P = 2L + 2W		Opposite sides equal

	Square	

Rectangle		Square
	Quadrilaterals	
Trapezoid		Parallelogram

	Trapezoid	

	Parallelogram	

50

Lotus

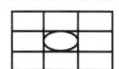

> **TIP**
>
> *Make the connections?*
>
> The lotus can be used to uncover commonalities and relationships. For example, after students have flushed out characteristics of all classes of vertebrates, they could use a highlighter to identify similarities in the different classes of animals.

Plugged Into Science?

How about a bit of probing to find out what your students already know about a topic? This teacher used the lotus diagram at the beginning of a new unit to assess just how much prior knowledge her kids had about vertebrates. After flushing out what they already knew and identifying the "gaps," she continued the lotus process to expand their knowledge—using her time wisely and strategically to uncover new ground, after having the kids cover old ground!

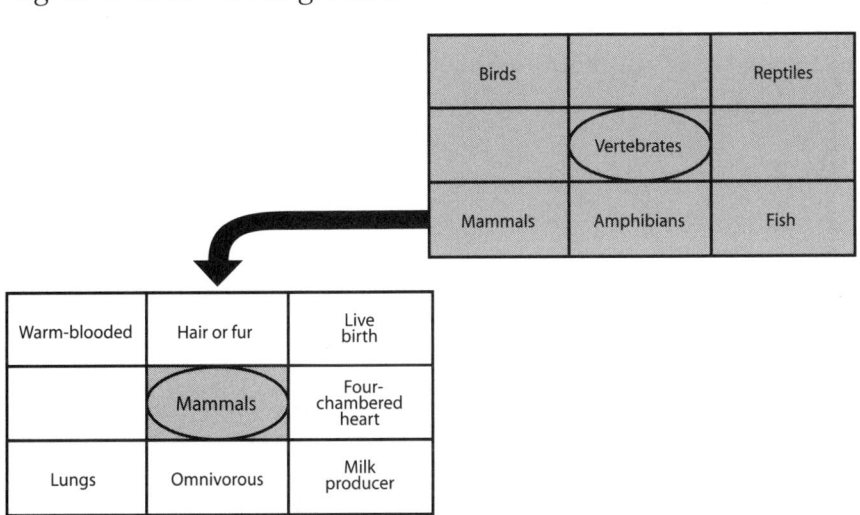

Birds		Reptiles
	Vertebrates	
Mammals	Amphibians	Fish

Warm-blooded	Hair or fur	Live birth
	Mammals	Four-chambered heart
Lungs	Omnivorous	Milk producer

> *To Flesh or To Flush? That is the question.*
>
> Flesh out as much detail as possible to fatten the fish. Or, flush out thoughts and facts . . . Like quails from the briar bush!

Chapter Two

Hollywood Lotus?

Smothers Brothers	Jo	Paul Lynde
Carolyn	Whoopi Goldberg	Janet
Kermit the Frog	Dr. Ruth	Charo

Whoopi Goldberg for the win! No, Carolyn. No, Janet. Oh heck, . . . Jo for the win!

Yes, in real life we are squares . . . without a doubt.

How About Writing?

How often have you heard a kid say, "But I don't know what to write!" This famous and familiar line disappears when you encourage your students to use a lotus diagram to organize and plan their writing. The lotus is user friendly—diminishing "blank paper panic," freeing the kids up to think, plan . . . create!

The prompt for this piece of clarification writing was, "Choose your favorite month of the year. Give reasons to support your choice." Notice how the student took the center box to begin her introductory paragraph, and then used the surrounding boxes to create supporting narrative.

Lotus

Presents		
	Christmas	Birth of Jesus
	Christmas tree	

Christmas		Birthdays
	My favorite month is December	
Weather		School is out

We feed the birds and little animals		It snows
	Weather	We make snow cream
Everything is so clean and white		We build a snowman

TIP

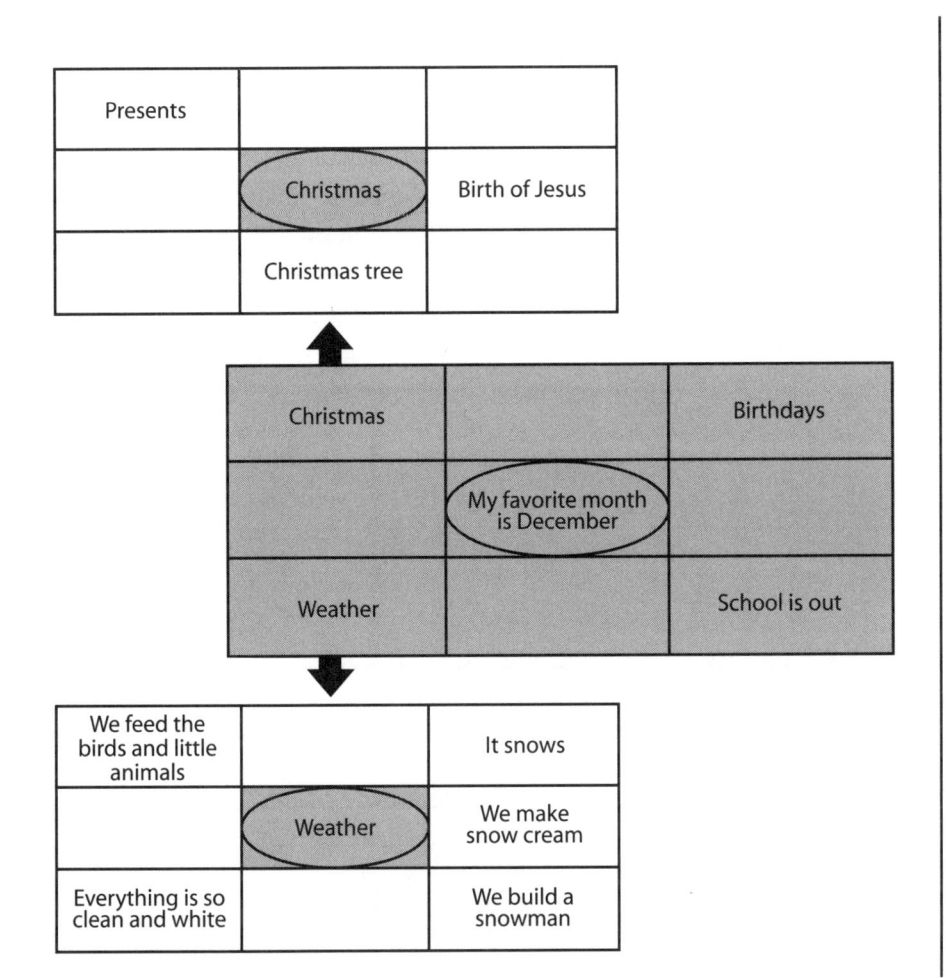

All those boxes confusing to younger kids?

Create a lotus by using different colored paper for each break-out box! Match topics with colors to help kids connect their ideas!

Students can also brainstorm a list of transition words and phrases they may want to use as they put all parts of their paper together! Imagine the many ways the lotus diagram can be used to facilitate and improve the writing process. Imagine the power of the lotus when preparing for writing assessments!

In conclusion,	By comparison,	Meanwhile,
Furthermore,	Transition Words & Phrases	However,
In addition,	Most significantly,	Of course,

> **TIP**
>
> Save time (and your eyes) by enlarging a blank lotus diagram. Laminate, use erasable markers, and use over and over again.

Lotus

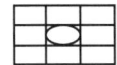

NOTES

Chapter Two

Think About It!

". . . Be dexterous and deft . . .
Out there things happen
And frequently do
To people as brainy
And footsy as you!"

Now really, how creative do you feel when you tell the kids to read the chapter and answer the textbook questions?

The lotus diagram is not only a lot more fun, but also a much more effective way of taking notes, summarizing, and reporting information—not to mention an excellent way to assess knowledge gained. Students can construct a lotus diagram (or two or three) on their own, as a team, or as a class. Be versatile. Be gutsy! Be footsy!

"You have the brains in your head
. . . feet in your shoes."

You can do it! So, do it!

Social Studies?

The lotus is an effective tool for uncovering the social studies curriculum and discovering history. Fourth graders across the country can use the lotus to uncover the history of their state: California kids can use the lotus to enrich their knowledge about Father Junipero Serra and mission life, the gold rush days, and the railroad. North Carolinians can explore pirates, Sir Walter Raleigh and the Lost Colony, and the Edenton Tea Party. Edenton Tea Party or the Boston Tea Party? Either and both! Of course, students can use the lotus to expand their knowledge and understanding of U.S. History, World History, Government, and Civics!

Legislative		Executive
	Branches of Government	
		Judicial

Lotus

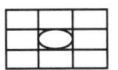

TIP

A completed lotus diagram holds a lot of information. Your eyes can get lost trying to see where to start!

Try shading the "beginning box" to make the starting point perfectly clear.

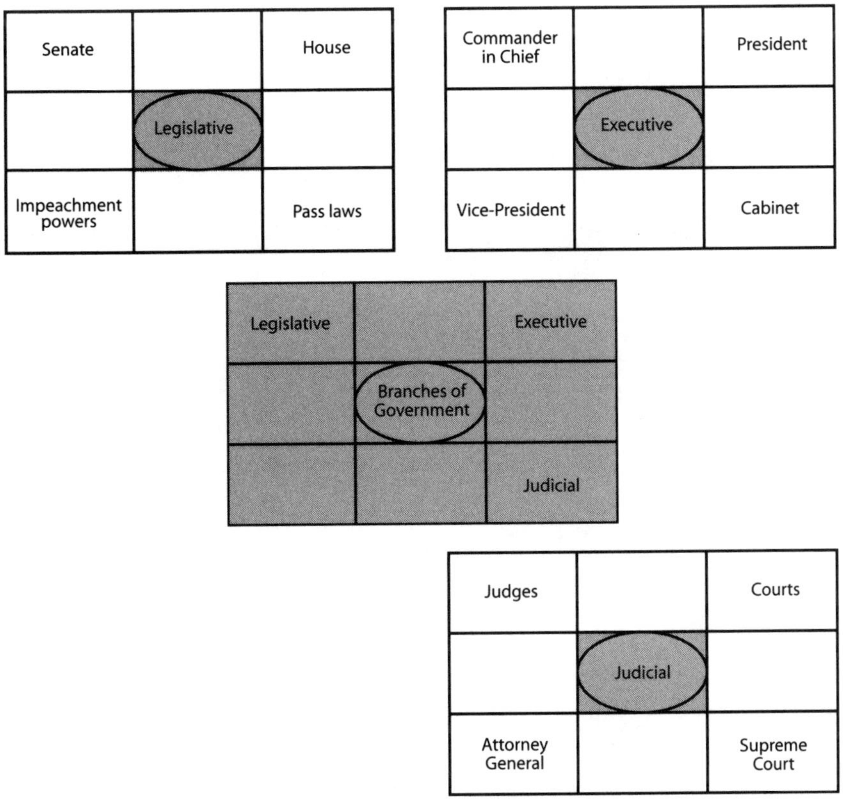

Senate		House
	Legislative	
Impeachment powers		Pass laws

Commander in Chief		President
	Executive	
Vice-President		Cabinet

Legislative		Executive
	Branches of Government	
		Judicial

Judges		Courts
	Judicial	
Attorney General		Supreme Court

57

Chapter Two

Like any other flower, a lotus continues to unfold, layer after layer. Look at the way these students can find and display more and more detailed information about the senate. Impressive, yes?

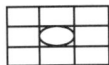

Plugging Into the Real World

. . . lotus diagrams help teachers plan too!

Schools are made up of many parts. As you know, there's a lot of planning that needs to be accomplished to ensure that all the parts are working together. A lotus can be used to help an entire school work together to make things run smoothly. For example:

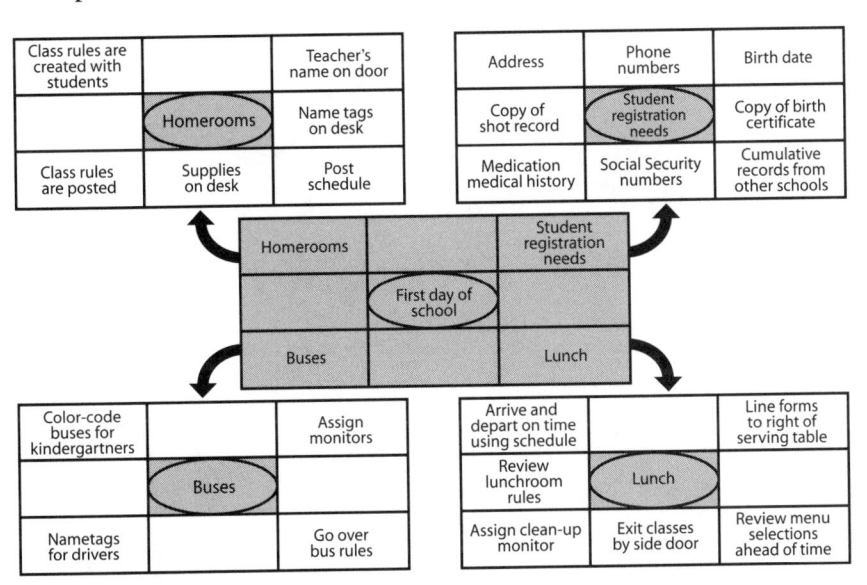

Class rules are created with students		Teacher's name on door
	Homerooms	Name tags on desk
Class rules are posted	Supplies on desk	Post schedule

Address	Phone numbers	Birth date
Copy of shot record	Student registration needs	Copy of birth certificate
Medication medical history	Social Security numbers	Cumulative records from other schools

Homerooms		Student registration needs
	First day of school	
Buses		Lunch

Color-code buses for kindergartners		Assign monitors
	Buses	
Nametags for drivers		Go over bus rules

Arrive and depart on time using schedule		Line forms to right of serving table
Review lunchroom rules	Lunch	
Assign clean-up monitor	Exit classes by side door	Review menu selections ahead of time

59

Chapter Two

TRY THE TIC-TAC-TOE APPROACH!

	Circulatory System	

	Musculo-skeletal System	

Circulatory		Musculo-skeletal
	Body Systems	
Respiratory		Nervous

	Respiratory System	

	Nervous System	

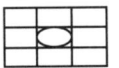

BE CREATIVE—HAVE FUN!

Alliteration
- Buzzing bees
- ...While I nodded nearly napping
- Rippling rapids
- All Amy's aunts are active!

Hyperbole
- We caught a fish as big as a truck.

Techniques authors use in their writing
- Humor
- Alliteration
- Metaphors
- Hyperbole
- Onomatopoeia
- Personification

Onomatopoeia
- Pop!
- Hiss!
- Snap!
- Thud!
- Bang!
- Buzz!

Personification
- The bird cried out, "Stop!"
- The fish were quarreling with each other.

Chapter Two

CURRICULUM IDEAS FROM A TO Z

LANGUAGE ARTS

- Types of punctuation
- Editing marks
- Story elements
- Types of figurative language
- Genres we've read
- Types of poetry
- Parts of speech
- Main ideas and supporting details
- Character analysis (name of character in center)
- Elements of a research paper

MATH

- Shapes
- Fractions and decimals
- Ways to illustrate numbers
- Money
- Time
- Temperature
- One to one correspondence
- Number words and numbers
- Conic sections
- Trigonometric ratios
- Ways to solve linear systems

SOCIAL STUDIES

- Ways communities use resources
- Patriotic symbols
- Examples of taxes
- How people have adapted to a hemisphere
- Causes of misuse of the environment
- Types of ethical and moral dilemmas
- Kinds of traditions
- Types of economic dependence
- The United Nations
- Great Britain (or any other nation)

GUIDANCE

- Ways we can work together
- Ways I am unique
- Feeling words
- Rules for participating in group discussions
- Good listening skills
- Consequences of my behavior
- Ways to show respect
- Different kinds of families

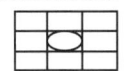

CURRICULUM IDEAS FROM A TO Z

SCIENCE

- Types of soil
- How we measure weather
- Animal environments
- Plant environments
- Kinds of matter
- Forms of energy
- Types of biological hazards
- Ways plants reproduce
- How things move
- Causes of changes in the weather
- Kingdoms of living things
- Phases of matter

HEALTH

- Types of health risks
- Ways to avoid sun exposure
- Kinds of first aid
- Ways to prevent tooth decay
- Sources of support to reduce stress
- Food guide pyramid
- Food safety rules
- Types of substance abuse
- Sexually transmitted diseases
- Risks of alcohol and drugs during pregnancy
- Fad diets

VOCATIONS & THE ARTS

- Musical genres
- Types of dances
- Painters
- Careers in health care, business, etc.
- Parts of a computer
- Parenting responsibilities

Chapter Two

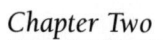

NOTES

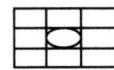

NOTES

To Kill a Mockingbird
Scout
Independent, Clear Thinker,
Courageous
Racism,
Social change,
conflicts
Atticus
father, wise,
trial
Coming of age
friendships, values,
taking a stand
Boo Radley
Misconceptions,
Isolation
Calpurnia
Mother figure,
maid

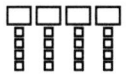

CHAPTER THREE

AFFINITY DIAGRAM

Why Use an Affinity Diagram to Uncover My Curriculum?

Uncovering the curriculum is a complex undertaking... and the affinity diagram is a robust process just right for the job! The affinity diagram is an idea-generating technique that kicks kids into innovative thinking—encouraging them to tap into their data banks, recall the facts they've learned, explore concepts they have been taught... to think inside and outside the box, investigate connections and affinities—both new and old.

The affinity is based on the brainstorming process and is a great way to get lots of ideas out and documented in a short amount of time. And, because all ideas are good ideas, kids love it and feel free to contribute. Everyone is successful... everyone is smart!

But, the affinity process is beyond brainstorming! Yes, it is an idea generating technique and taps into the "right brain."

But this technique also taps into the "left brain" as it involves the kids in methodical reflection, analyzing, organizing, and categorizing.

Chapter Three

You learned how to facilitate this process in *Future Force* (pp. 50-54), so you're ready, let's go . . . it's time to plug it right into your curriculum!

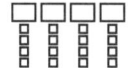

Plugging Into Culture, Foreign Language, or Foreign Literature!

> "... *Si, mis amigos y estudiantes ... aloha ...
> je voudrais un pomme de terre ... ciao!*"

So, what's anything and everything your kids know about France? Everyone is invited to contribute . . . all ideas are invited and welcome—from favorite foods, geographical facts, tourist tidbits, historical moments, politics, and sights to see. You can use this tool to introduce a topic and see how much and what they already know, or to take class notes, assimilate a chapter or two, or to create a student-made study guide for a quiz, a midterm, a final, or a high-stakes proficiency exam.

This first set of ideas is an example of the free-wheeling idea-generating phase.

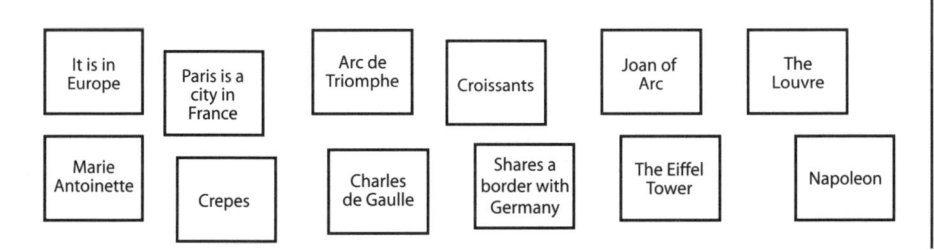

| It is in Europe | Paris is a city in France | Arc de Triomphe | Croissants | Joan of Arc | The Louvre |
| Marie Antoinette | Crepes | Charles de Gaulle | Shares a border with Germany | The Eiffel Tower | Napoleon |

TIP

- Kids can brainstorm ideas on sticky notes and post them on chart paper, the board, a wall, the floor, or wherever!

- New ideas can be added at any time during the process—really! New ideas are welcome . . . whatever, whenever!

- Stick-on posting notes are certainly the most convenient, but note cards or bits of paper and a little tape will do the job—just as long as the ideas can be moved around and about until they find their home.

Chapter Three

This data is beginning to look categorized . . . but what's the nature of the category?

Joan of Arc	Croissants	Arc de Triomphe	Paris is a city in France
Napoleon	Crepes	The Louvre	Shares a border with Germany
Charles de Gaulle		The Eiffel Tower	It is in Europe
Marie Antoinette			

Affinity

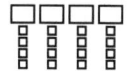

This data set displays the final product—ideas categorized into natural affinities and labeled to boot!

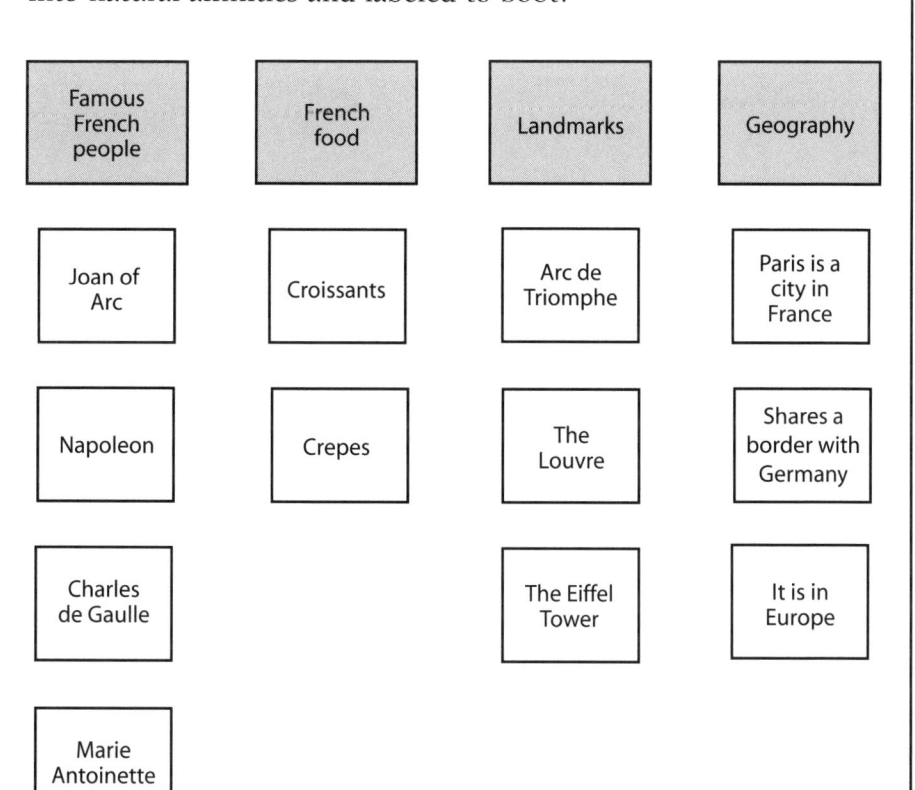

Famous French people	French food	Landmarks	Geography
Joan of Arc	Croissants	Arc de Triomphe	Paris is a city in France
Napoleon	Crepes	The Louvre	Shares a border with Germany
Charles de Gaulle		The Eiffel Tower	It is in Europe
Marie Antoinette			

DEFINITION

An affinity is an attraction, likeness, or close resemblance.

That's how these ideas have been grouped!

Chapter Three

> **Don't You Dare!**
>
> - Don't even be tempted to give your students the categories!
>
> - The power of this tool is to begin harem-scare'em with freewheeling brainstorming—that's right, no preset categories.
>
> - Discussion comes next—unbridled by traditional structure.
>
> - Categories are the last step—ensuring innovative thinking and a new twist to an old tale.

Plugged Into Reading

Kids of all ages can use this tool to capture what they've read, to analyze and synthesize—whether preparing a book report, getting ready for an oral report, or gearing up for a quiz! Plot, setting, characters . . . uncover it all. Again, it's think, think, and think again. Not a bad idea, huh?

Affinity

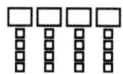

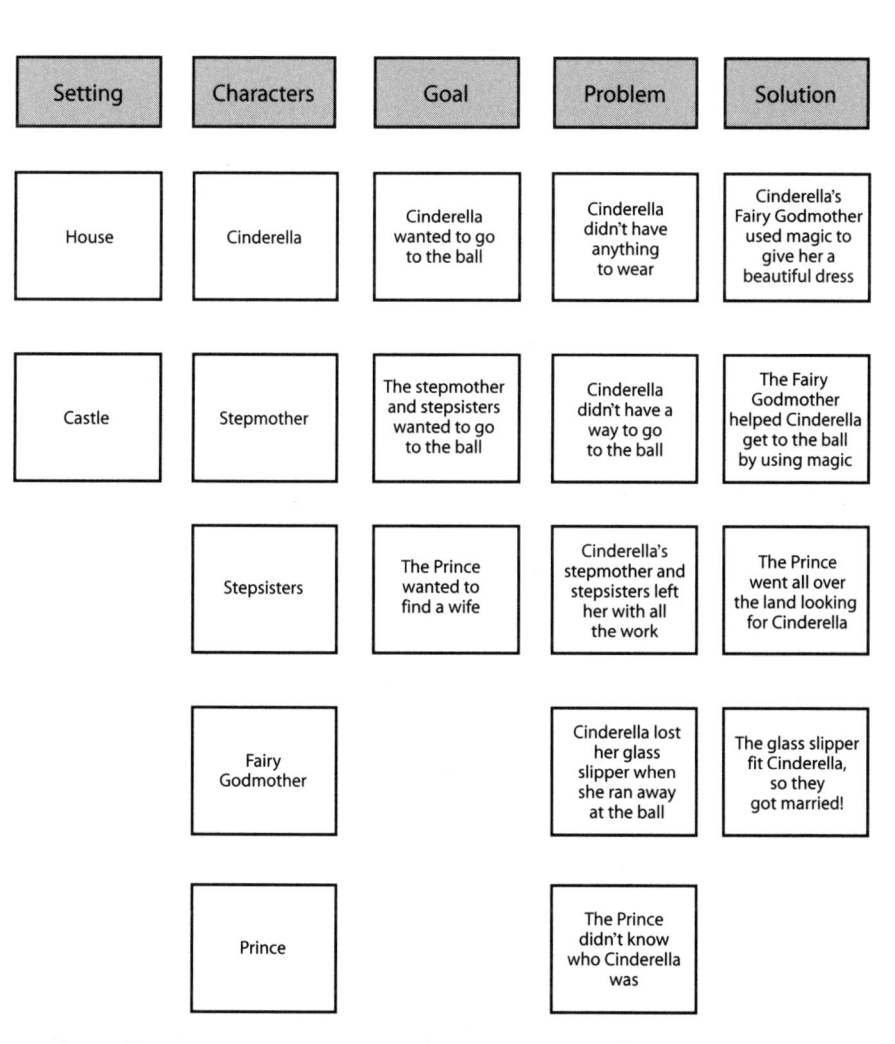

Setting	Characters	Goal	Problem	Solution
House	Cinderella	Cinderella wanted to go to the ball	Cinderella didn't have anything to wear	Cinderella's Fairy Godmother used magic to give her a beautiful dress
Castle	Stepmother	The stepmother and stepsisters wanted to go to the ball	Cinderella didn't have a way to go to the ball	The Fairy Godmother helped Cinderella get to the ball by using magic
	Stepsisters	The Prince wanted to find a wife	Cinderella's stepmother and stepsisters left her with all the work	The Prince went all over the land looking for Cinderella
	Fairy Godmother		Cinderella lost her glass slipper when she ran away at the ball	The glass slipper fit Cinderella, so they got married!
	Prince		The Prince didn't know who Cinderella was	

This affinity was done by itty bitty kiddies! Bibbidi, bobbidi, boo!

Chapter Three

NOTES

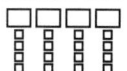

Science—Rigorous and Plugged In!

Scientists at all age and grade levels—not to mention physicists, geologists, or chemists in the professional world—can and do use the affinity diagram to get their ideas out and start the planning process. The real beauty of this tool is the process itself, but the final document is worthy in its own right and can be used to communicate complex concepts, processes, and plans.

These kids titled the top of their chart, "What's the Matter with Matter?" Then the ideas began to flow . . . solids, liquids, and gases—oh my!

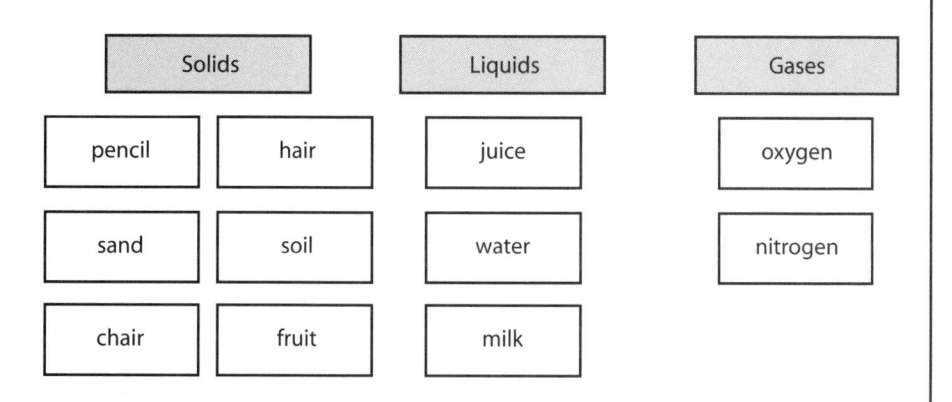

Solids		Liquids	Gases
pencil	hair	juice	oxygen
sand	soil	water	nitrogen
chair	fruit	milk	

What Do You Think?

Did the teacher come up with the headers for this affinity? Heck no!

These second graders first generated any and all thoughts about the matter around them, and then through rigorous second-grade dialogue, merged them into natural affinities (which happened to match scientific categories).

Plugged Into the Arts

"I've got rhythm . . . I've got music . . ."
I've got my ideas, who could ask for anything more?

Yes, you can use this tool to collect, categorize, and convey information in visual arts, dramatic arts, music, and more. The following example comes from a team of students preparing for auditions. Just what are the criteria for an excellent vocal performance?

Affinity

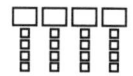

> **TIP**
>
> *This affinity diagram could be used to develop a rubric for vocal performance.*
>
> Students who have a rubric and know the criteria can produce quality work!

Volume	Expression and Style	Rhythm and Pitch	Voice Quality
Be sure to sing loud enough	Facial expression matches the mood of music	Stay on pitch	Voice sounds pleasing
Don't sing too loud	Style that fits the piece of music	Rhythm is correct	Pleasant voice tone
You have to be heard over the accompaniment	Engage listeners		
	Look at the audience		

Chapter Three

> **Challenge!**
>
> - What is Bloom's Taxonomy?
>
> - What is the Application Model, and how can it be used with Bloom's Taxonomy to help teachers create rigorous and relevant real-world problem-solving opportunities for students?
>
> - What is Authentic Assessment, and who pioneered the concept of backward design in creating these assessments?

Plugged Into the Real World

Problem Solving—Math, Science, Communication . . .

Integrated learning? You bet. Any and all of these tools can be used to integrate learning in math, science, history, communication, and everything else in order to confront and solve real-world problems effectively and efficiently. The affinity diagram is a great place to start—generating ideas to innovate and think outside the box . . . to conquer new territory, come up with groundbreaking concepts.

Think about this: Instead of telling your kids how to approach the problem and supplying a series of tasks or questions, why not turn them loose and let them investigate and create their own problem-solving strategy! Creating the future force . . . launching the thinkers and doers that will take us into the future . . . planning and preparing for tomorrow.

In the following example you will see how the tool plugs directly into the curriculum, and the curriculum plugs into the real world.

Affinity

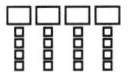

> ***Remember!***
>
> Sheet-rocking is back, but this time with new purpose and process!

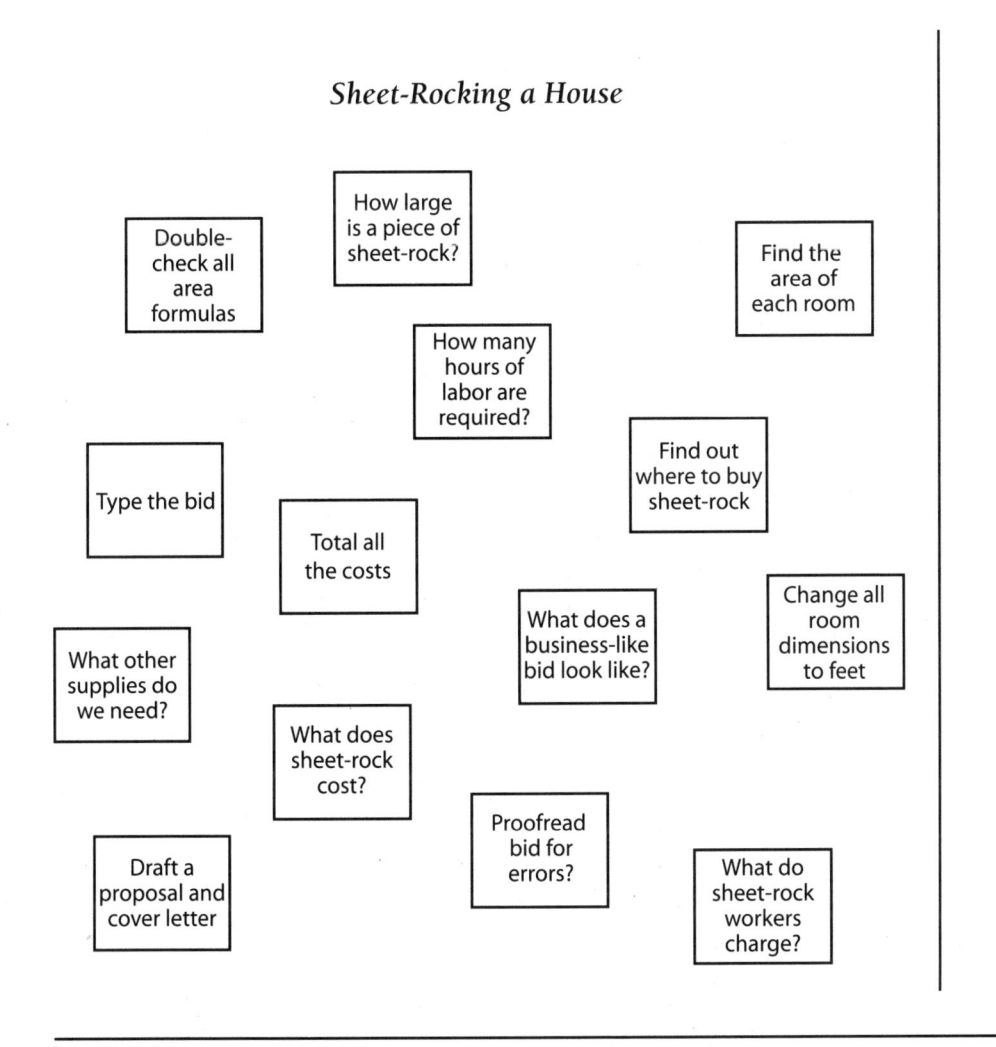

Sheet-Rocking a House

- Double-check all area formulas
- How large is a piece of sheet-rock?
- Find the area of each room
- How many hours of labor are required?
- Type the bid
- Find out where to buy sheet-rock
- Total all the costs
- Change all room dimensions to feet
- What other supplies do we need?
- What does a business-like bid look like?
- What does sheet-rock cost?
- Draft a proposal and cover letter
- Proofread bid for errors?
- What do sheet-rock workers charge?

Chapter Three

Put it together and what do you get . . . bibbidi, bobbidi, boo? No, the stuff that moves students from first steps right into action!

Math Computations	Supply Costs	Labor Costs	Communication with Customer
Change all room dimensions to feet	Find out where to buy sheet-rock	What do sheet-rock workers charge?	What does a business-like bid look like?
Find the area of each room	How large is a piece of sheet-rock?	How many hours of labor are required?	Type the bid
Double-check all area formulas	What does sheet-rock cost?		Proofread bid for errors?
Total all the costs	What other supplies do we need?		Draft a proposal and cover letter

Affinity

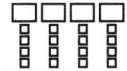

This innovative and up-to-date teacher turned the kids loose to investigate, then stood back as they translated their exploration into an action plan that led to success!

Action Plan		
What	**Who**	**By When**
Double-check formulas	Team	4-10
Where to buy sheet-rock?	Tina	4-11
What does sheet-rock cost?	Joe	4-12
What do workers charge?	Melissa	4-11
How many hours of labor?	Steven	4-12
Total all the costs	Team	4-13
Type the bid	Tina	4-14
Draft proposal and cover letter	Team	4-14

Chapter Three

How Do I Use an Affinity for Assessment?

As the day for your final assessment (the dreaded test) approaches, why not use the affinity process to pre-assess your students' current understanding?

In the following example, teams of students worked together to respond to the question, "What's everything you know about World War I?" The teacher used the draft affinities to assess her students' current level of understanding, and then prepared learning activities to correct misinformation and fill in the gaps before the final test. The kids were studying for the test in an interactive, free-from-stress way that involved the entire class. Better yet, the completed affinities became student-made study guides visibly displayed for the entire class. This affinity was huge! A few of their great ideas are shown on the following page. Other categories included People, Types of Warfare, and Aftermath.

Affinity

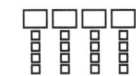

Causes of Start of War (1914)	Causes of American Entry into War	Weapons
Militarism	Zimmerman note	Airplanes
Nationalism	Sinking of the Lusitania	Chemical weapons
Franz Ferdinand assassinated	Freedom of the seas	Machine guns
Imperialism		Tanks
Secret Alliances		Submarines

TIP

- Whether a student is five, ten, or eighteen, in first grade or twelfth, kids are proud of their work.
- Show it off!
- Put the finished product on a bulletin board or wall for everyone to see.
- Share the wealth—share the learning!

Chapter Three

CURRICULUM IDEAS FROM A TO Z

LANGUAGE ARTS

- What do we need to include when writing in a specified mode?
- Techniques authors use to grab our interest
- What do complete sentences include?
- Supporting details from the story that led us to the main idea
- Sources of conflict in the story
- Examples of conflict in a specific novel or play
- What is everything you know about a specific novel, play, or story?

SCIENCE

- Types of plants
- Animal homes
- Things that float
- Things that sink
- Safety rules for using science equipment
- Forms of energy
- Causes of changes to the earth
- Causes of changes in weather
- Climate trends
- Causes of pollution

SOCIAL STUDIES

- Events that tell about our heritage
- Community workers
- Holidays and customs
- Community resources
- Reasons for economic interdependence in a community or region
- Good citizenship
- Reasons some communities disappeared
- What do we know about Africa?
- What do we know about the Korean War?

MUSIC

- Rules for using instruments
- Uses for music
- Rhythmic symbols
- Things to remember when evaluating a performance
- Different kinds of music
- Music from a historical period
- Things to remember when composing music

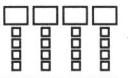

CURRICULUM IDEAS FROM A TO Z

HEALTH & P.E.

- Name as many drugs (prescription, non-prescription, illegal) as you can.
- Ways to lose weight
- Equipment needed for baseball (or any other sport)
- Types of exercise
- Rules for basketball (or any other game)
- Diseases
- Health hazards

VOCATIONS

- Computer components
- Jobs in the medical (or any other) field
- Tools and their uses
- Things to remember when writing a business letter
- Parts of an office memo
- Appropriate audiences for a presentation
- Procedures/guidelines for oral presentations

MATH

- Geometric shapes
- Properties of parallelograms
- Information about fractions
- Information about trigonometric ratios
- Ways to display data
- Things to remember when graphing a line
- Units of measurement
- Different kinds of shapes
- Probability guesses
- Pattern detecting
- Repeated addition

Keep those thoughts coming!

Chapter Three

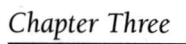

NOTES

Affinity

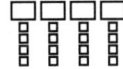

NOTES

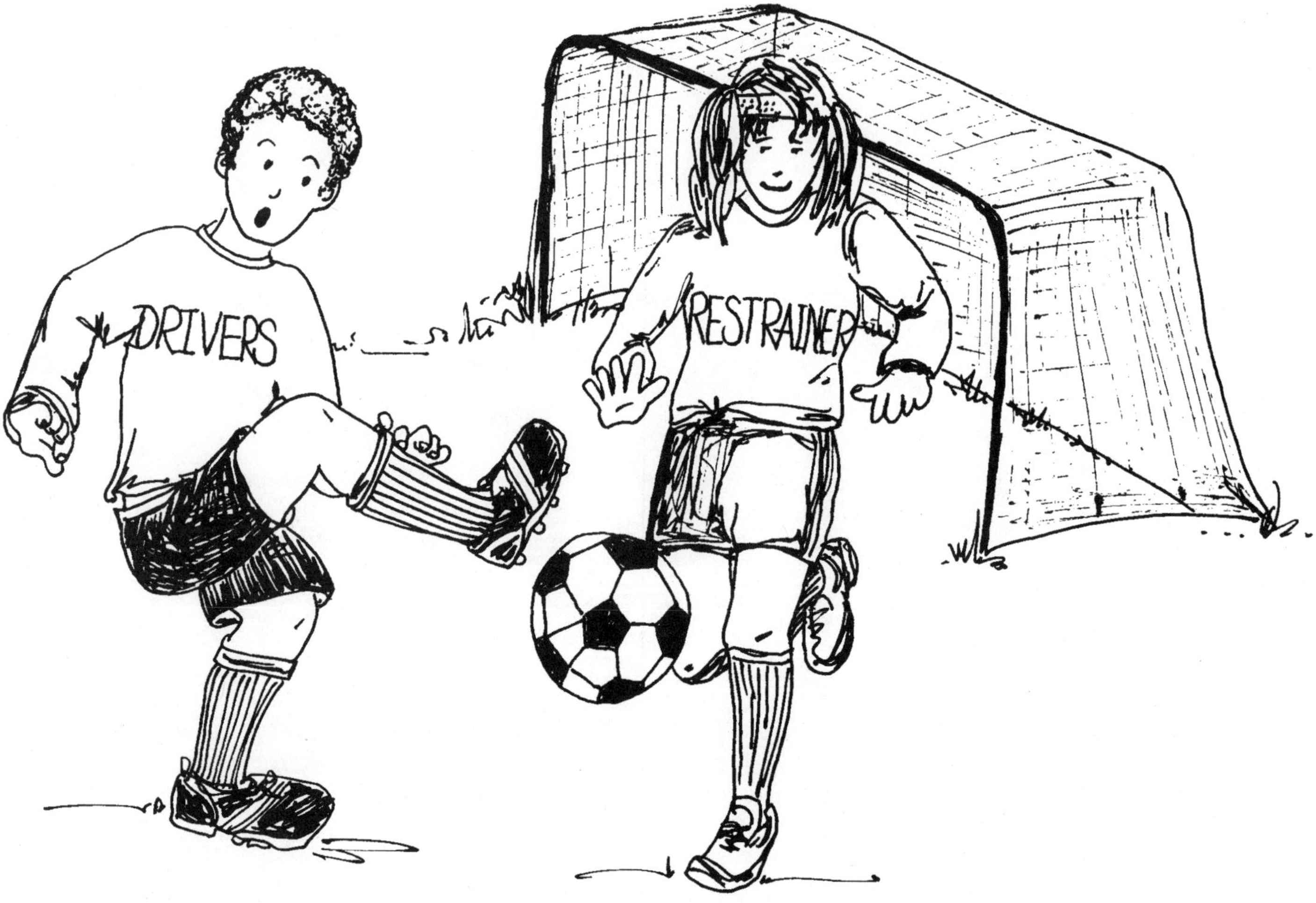
DRIVERS
RESTRAINER

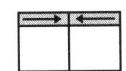

CHAPTER FOUR

FORCE FIELD ANALYSIS

Why Use a Force Field Analysis to Uncover My Curriculum?

> *"Do you dare stay out? Do you dare go in?*
> *How much can you lose? How much can you win?*
> *And if you go in, should you turn left or right . . .*
> *Or right-and-three-quarters? Or maybe not quite?"*

Simple it's not, we're afraid you will find, for mind-maker-uppers to make up their minds. But, and this is a big BUT! . . . they can do it, especially with the help of force field analysis. Now, you learned this tool in *Future Force* (pp. 60-61), but even if you hadn't, you could figure it out. Although this is without a doubt one of the most powerful quality tools in our bank of resources, it is also one of the simplest to use.

Force field analysis is a great exploratory and decision-making tool, encouraging great thinkers to think even more deeply, uncover more ground, and probe even further into the depths of critical and analytical reasoning to conquer the curriculum. Force field analysis helps kids develop their ability to think about the reasoning behind theories, philosophies, and hypotheses as well as events, situations, and decisions. As students engage

Chapter Four

in this process, they learn to consider the "driving forces" that initiate, strengthen, or drive while simultaneously processing the "restraining forces" that hinder, weaken, or block.

Now notice that we said "driving forces" and "restraining forces," and did not imply "either/or" dichotomous thinking. That's right, in virtually any situation dealing with almost any concept within your curriculum, both drivers and restrainers do exist . . . that goes in real life as well! Life is not absolute, not black and white. Decisions and positions are not always easily reached or taken: the key is to think, think, and think again. This technique encourages kids to challenge the complexity, become problem solvers with a depth of perspective to ground them in their stance.

So, yes . . . let the force be with you in your classroom as you uncover your curriculum!

Force Field

Plugged Into Math

Mathematical minds go far beyond the precision of calculations and the application of equations. Grounded with mathematical principles and skills, kids take their know-how and move into the problem-solving mode. In traditional classrooms with traditional texts, kids groan and moan, hem and haw, sharpen their pencils and scratch out their answers to page after page of skill sets and word problems—and of course they must and do show their work!

But in the real world there is not one right approach or one right answer. For example, if you asked three different contractors to give you a bid for sheet-rocking your house, would each contractor give you the exact same bid, the exact same timeline, the same products and process? Of course not! But couldn't each bid be right in its own right?

And, we're not suggesting that any or all of your kids will become sheet-rockers. But kids need the thinking skills necessary to become conscientious, well-informed, well-prepared consumers of bids, propositions, and the like. Kids need to learn the complexities of real-world problem solving, and the force field is an effective tool to take into the field of higher mathematics, as well as into the foundational stages of elementary math. Begin this kind of thinking in kindergarten, first, second, and third grade, and just imagine the places you'll go—the places we'll go—as our young mathematicians take us into the future.

Little Kids, Too!

Younger students . . . 5, 6 and 7 year-olds . . . can use force field analysis to ponder the drivers and restrainers of spending their allowance, cost of pet care, class parties, picnics and the like.

Check out the examples provided at the end of the chapter to see ways to help little folks plug in!

Chapter Four

Can you visualize the various force field diagrams created by the high school sheet-rocking teams? Fun and inspiring, don't ya' think? This kind of thinking is not limited to the world of work, but also to the everyday problems that we all encounter routinely and continuously. Following is an example developed by a student who was tasked with the real-world problem of buying a car. The challenges ranged from dream car expectations to real for sure pocket books, to insurance requirements.

Buying the Older Car	
Drivers →	← Restrainers
• I can afford to buy it now	• It is not as reliable as a newer car
• I don't need a loan to buy it	• It is not as "cool" as a new car
• Having no car payments gives me money for other things	• I need to do some work on it before I can drive it
• No need for collision insurance due to age of car	• There is no warranty in case repairs are needed

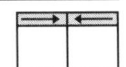

Is there a third alternative? Is there an option that lies somewhere between a Porsche, a 4x4 SUV, and a rattletrap Studebaker?

In another classroom, teams of kids were tasked to compare the various plans available from rental car companies at a local airport. In this simulation task, the students were asked to pretend that they worked for a travel agency and needed to be prepared to recommend the best options for a diverse group of customers. The students used the force field to look at the drivers and restrainers per each rental car company. Talk about exploring the variability of the competitive market!

Were these kids up to the task at hand? At one point their teacher questioned whether this task was too complex, too challenging, and perhaps overwhelming. She wondered if she had gone overboard. But fortunately she kept her doubts to herself. The kids explored the ins and outs and ups and downs of this marketplace without becoming overwhelmed or discouraged. In fact, they enjoyed their foray into the real world! And, why not? They were armed with tools and processes to problem solve just as effectively—or more so—than real, live people. Hey! Students are real, live people, yes?

> **CHALLENGE**
>
> What are Langford teams and how do they relate to real-world problem solving?

The Road Not Taken

Two roads diverged in a yellow wood,
And sorry I could not travel both
And be one traveler, long I stood
And looked down one as far as I could
To where it bent in the undergrowth,

Then took the other, as just as fair,
And having perhaps the better claim,
Because it was grassy and wanted wear,
Though as for that the passing there
Had worn them really about the same,

And both that morning equally lay
In leaves no step had trodden black.
Oh, I kept the first for another day!
Yet knowing how way leads on to way,
I doubted if I should ever come back.

I shall be telling this with a sigh
Somewhere ages and ages hence:
Two roads diverged in a wood, and I—
I took the one less traveled by,
And that has made all the difference.

by Robert Frost

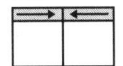

Plugged Into Poetry . . . And Why Not?!

When traveling down the road with your kids on the road not taken, a road less taken, or tripping down the cobble stones, or following the yellow brick road . . . a force field analysis can and will help you and your kids to explore the depths of poetry and any and all literature. *Island of the Blue Dolphins*? You bet. *All Quiet on the Western Front*? Of course. *Roll of Thunder, Hear My Cry*? Absolutely and without a doubt! In the following example, you will see how the force field helped these kids to analyze "The Road Not Taken," by Robert Frost.

Choosing the Less Traveled Road	
Drivers →	← Restrainers
• Challenge	• Fear of failure
• Opportunity	• Peer pressure
• Leadership	• Fear of the unknown
• Curiosity	• Laziness
• Possible reward	• Fear of being alone
• Nonconformity	• Conformity

Teachers, Take A Look!

Take a look at the "Choosing the Less Traveled Road" force field. Do these very restrainers sometimes stop you in your tracks, stop you as a teacher from taking a new road, tackling a change, trying a new tool?

Chapter Four

Social Studies, History, Civilization . . .

Think about the driving and restraining forces experienced throughout time. Would history be changed if our ancestors or forefathers had used the force field to confront challenges and make decisions? Okay, a bit audacious on our part . . . but . . . maybe . . . perhaps??? Just a little brain tickler to see if you're still on your toes, with your feet in your shoes!

But seriously, the force field is a powerful process to use as youngsters explore the forces met from the beginning of civilization to the launching of the Niña, Pinta, and Santa Maria to the first toes entering Valley Forge to the crumbling of the Berlin Wall. Whether studying tribes of Indians struggling to adapt to their environment or senators and representatives filibustering to block the floor, force field analysis is a powerful way to open the eyes and minds of our young students. The following example demonstrates the way a team of students investigated the drivers and restrainers of different tribes adapting to their environment, while another example displays an individual student's analysis of what drove and what inhibited immigrants as they considered a rigorous trek. Can you believe that the force fields produced to explore the drivers and restrainers confronted by immigrants to our country led to a spontaneous, lively, and in-depth dialogue about going to a new school? Got our attention, how about yours?

Force Field

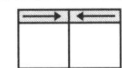

Tribe A	
Drivers →	← Restrainers

Tribe B	
Drivers →	← Restrainers

Tribe C	
Drivers →	← Restrainers

Immigrating to America	
Drivers →	← Restrainers
• Religious freedom	• Language barriers
• Escape oppression	• Low-paying jobs
• Economic opportunity	• Facing prejudice in America
• Social equality	• Fear of leaving home

Chapter Four

Can you imagine how students can translate their learning from the historical past into the here-and-now realities of today? Take a look at how these kindergarten kids explore the basics of good citizenship . . . from young minds to higher-level learning . . . the beginnings of understanding . . . the vast discrepancies and perspectives between structure and chaos, freedom and responsibility.

Being A Good Citizen In Our Neighborhood	
What would help us GO forward →	**What would STOP us?** ←
• Following rules • Putting our trash in trash cans • Helping other people	• Breaking rules • Throwing trash on the ground

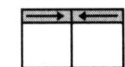

NOTES

Chapter Four

To Your Health and Health Science!

Although the force field is not the best tool for freewheeling brainstorming, it is without a doubt one of the most powerful tools for encouraging higher-level thinking—challenging kids to explore issues through thoughtful analysis of driving and restraining forces and the complex interactions between. The following example deals with the drivers and restrainers of fad diets—a healthy start to investigating health and nutrition in relationship to the hosts of quick and easy diets that flood our culture—diets complete with fun buzz words, fashion, and pop stars promising not only thinner thighs in thirty days but popularity and glamour to boot!

As you look at the fad diet example provided, imagine the power of using this tool to analyze the forces that drive fad diets and challenging them with the restraining forces that may impede or dissuade a quick-fix approach.

Through force field analysis, kids learn to embrace diverse perspectives, positions, and beliefs, challenge their own stance or the stance of others, the simple solutions, and then work to come to terms with complexity—conquering group think as they move beyond the concrete and obvious to contemplate long-term and systemic alternatives.

Force Field

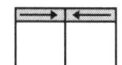

Fad Diets	
Drivers →	← Restrainers
• Quick weight loss	• No long-term weight loss
• Easy	• May be dangerous to health
• Short-term	• May not be nutritionally balanced
• Money back guarantee	

Chapter Four

> *Plugged Into Environmental Science . . .*
>
> Absolutely! Whether grasping scientific theory, challenging hypotheses, or confronting experimental design, force field analysis engages students in thoughtful consideration and rigorous dialogue, providing students with a pathway to higher learning, launching kids into the scientific method.
>
> Across the country, science standards are emphasizing environmental issues. A team of middle schoolers created the following example as they journeyed into the rain forest to explore ecological systems. The force field not only helped these kids explore systemic interactions, but also helped to prepare them for standardized assessment.

Force Field

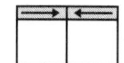

Preserving Rain Forests	
Drivers →	← Restrainers
• Desire to avoid extinction of species • Medical research possibilities • Aesthetic value • Environmental value	• Overpopulation • Industrial expansion • Lack of understanding • Apathy

Chapter Four

> **An Interactive Force Field?**
>
> A young speaker can use a blank force field diagram to solicit input from the audience, engaging them in interaction at a level that energizes the exchange.

Plugged Into Public Speaking . . .

Force field analysis is a great way to prepare for any type of public speaking—speeches, debates, or dynamic presentations designed to engage the audience as interactive participants. Public speaking of any nature always begins with gathering your thoughts together. The force field provides a process to help your students delve into the depths and complexity of any issue. Any good debater knows that knowing both sides of the coin, knowing the drivers and restrainers, is a critical part of the preparation process. Think how often English teachers remind us that in persuasive writing or speaking, to be effective one must consider the opposing perspectives. That's exactly what the force field process does. And, better yet, the final product is not only well-prepared young minds, but a visual display of the hard-earned, complex thoughts to boot! This compilation of thoughts can be used as visual support to assist the speaker, while providing the audience with visual stimuli.

Check out the following example, and then give the force field a try . . . you'll like it!

Force Field

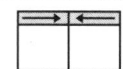

A Quality Oral Presentation	
Drivers →	← Restrainers
• Speaking clearly	• Mumbling
• Speaking loud enough for everyone to hear	• Bad posture
• Standing up straight	• Not looking at your audience
• Eye contact with the audience	• Playing with something in your hands

Assessment! Yet another powerful way to use the force field.

TIP

Teachers, students, and professionals in all arenas have found that using the quality tools in tandem set them up for success—from oral reports, to stand-up speeches, to formal presentations and proposals.

Just imagine using an affinity diagram to generate, synthesize, and categorize ideas. Then, how about taking the header cards right off the affinity diagram, moving into the interrelationship diagram (*Future Force*, pp. 75-79), and then onto a bone diagram (*Plugged In*, Chapter 6), a force field . . . followed up by an action plan. Can't get any better than that!

Again, you move through a thinking process that results not only in a wealth of ideas and a depth of perspective, but also visual proof of your efforts—visual proof that can be used to assist any individual or team present their work. And yes, audiences appreciate visual aids to help them track!

105

Chapter Four

Plugged Into Assessment

Assessment is really about goals and monitoring your progress toward those goals. An important part of being able to reach one's goals is to identify what's going to help get you there, and what might hold you back or get in the way. Yep, it's a matter of identifying the driving forces and the restraining forces. Oh, the power of force field analysis!

Students who were in the process of proposing student-led conferences in lieu of the traditional parent-teacher approach created the following example.

Force Field

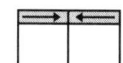

Student-Led Conference	
Drivers →	**← Restrainers**
• Student accountability • Pride of workmanship • Straight from the horse's mouth • Increased parent involvement • Improves communication between parent and child • Improves student presentation skills • Builds leadership mindset and skills • Requires cooperation and communication between teacher and student	• Goes against tradition • Teachers might view as more work for them • Teachers feel loss of control • Possible parent concerns • Seems like it could be more time consuming • Makes students nervous • Requires cooperation and communication between teacher and student

CHALLENGE

- What is the Effective Schools Movement?

- What are the Effective Schools Correlates?

- Who is Larry Lezotte?

107

CURRICULUM IDEAS FROM A TO Z

LANGUAGE ARTS

- Complete sentences
- A great opening paragraph
- A great closing paragraph
- Analyzing story events, character actions, conflict, problems, and solutions
- Making informed judgments about television/film/video productions
- Impact of literary elements on a piece of writing
- Considering alternative points of view
- Use of certain technological and informational resources for a particular piece of research
- Examining the theme of a piece of literature

HEALTH & P.E.

- Taking medication to control cholesterol levels
- Using legal body-building substances
- Taking supplements to "bulk up" for certain sports
- Dieting to reach weight limitations in certain sports
- Moderate alcohol consumption

SCIENCE

- Types of plants
- Animal homes
- Things that float
- Things that sink
- Safety rules for using science equipment
- Forms of energy
- Causes of changes to the earth
- Causes of changes in weather
- Climate trends
- Causes of pollution
- Protecting endangered species
- Organisms adapting to certain environments
- Vision loss
- Land runoff
- Preserving rain forests
- Developing alternative energy sources
- Developing genetically engineered foods
- Using pesticides in farming
- Using weather satellites to predict the weather
- Placing wild animals in zoos
- Using plastics
- Conserving energy and resources

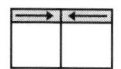

CURRICULUM IDEAS FROM A TO Z

SOCIAL STUDIES

- Misuse of our environment
- Use our resources
- Good citizenship
- To follow rules
- Traditions
- Higher taxes
- Selection of certain leaders
- America's entrance into World War I
- Ending apartheid in South Africa
- An elected leader's failure to gain re-election
- An explorer's choice of route in an exploration of unknown territory
- Scarcity of goods and services
- Adoption of certain traditions in various cultures
- Why people in different countries eat certain foods

GUIDANCE

- Working together
- Good decisions
- Good listeners
- Solve our problems

ARTS

- Artist's choice of medium and style
- A good performance
- Appropriate choice of music for an event
- A culture's expression of dance as a ritual
- Good backstage behavior

May the force be with you!

Chapter Four

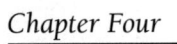

NOTES

Force Field

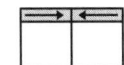

NOTES

Chapter Five

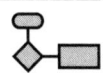

CHAPTER FIVE

FLOWCHART DIAGRAM

Flowcharting the Curriculum . . . A Flow of Its Own!

Flowcharts can be plugged into math, English, or science, as well as into music, art, or any other subject. Flowcharts can map out or sequence the stages of a project, the steps of a problem, the phases of any story, situation, or event . . . and the power is not just that the flowchart does this so clearly and efficiently, but rather that it transforms these events, phases, and stages into processes—introducing and reinforcing process thinking, one of the basic tenets of Total Quality.

What is process thinking and why is it important? Process thinking is viewing activities, tasks, or plans with a systemic perspective. Process thinking helps kids learn to realize how ideas, decisions, and actions impact each other. Recognizing events and activities as a process helps kids learn to start breaking down assignments and complex topics into related tasks and activities that move toward the final goal or fill in the big picture.

Chapter Five

> ### What Is a People Coordinate?
>
> *Remember graphing points and lines in high school algebra class?*
>
> *Remember how there was always an x-coordinate and a y-coordinate?*
>
> In a deployment flowchart, there is a people coordinate so that the flowchart can show not only the sequence of events, but also the people who are involved in each step of the process.
>
> *Clever, efficient, and effective, huh?*

The flowchart is just the tool to plug process thinking right into the curriculum. While some tools uncover the curriculum, the flowchart maps it out. The flowchart maps sequence through the flow of symbols, plots out the key stakeholders in the people coordinate, and identifies quality issues pertinent to the task at hand. But more than just delineating sequence and identifying components, students learn to identify decision points, forecast dilemmas or challenges, plan contingencies, and build quality thinking right into the process.

So, step back, take a breath, and remember that the curriculum is yours and your students'. While adults do indeed determine what the learning objectives are, the students can have input into the how. Just think, while your students use flowcharting to map out the core content and learning processes of your shared curriculum, they'll once again be developing skills that tackle real-world problems.

You learned how to flowchart in *Future Force* (pp. 69-72), so brush up on those symbols and start charting your way through the curriculum.

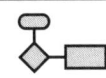

NOTES

Plugged Into Math

Can you think of a subject with as many processes that need to be learned and remembered as in math? Math teachers everywhere give kids the "rules" to follow as they try to conquer the processes for mathematical operations at every level. Too often, kids don't make the connection, can't remember, or can't apply to the next concept.

Teachers assign the work, then as the students do the work, they sometimes encounter trouble—"What do I do? What is the next step?" When this happens, the kid's hand pops up, and the expectation is that the teacher will walk right over and "put them back on the right track." A flowchart helps kids visualize the math processes and remember the steps in the operation, and it can be helpful in planning any type of problem solving.

So, save yourself a few steps and have the kids map out the steps in a graphical display that is visibly dynamic! With the flowchart as a guide, the students can keep themselves on the right track as they practice—that is, until they don't need it anymore because the process has been internalized.

Multiplying Positive and Negative Numbers

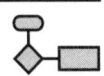

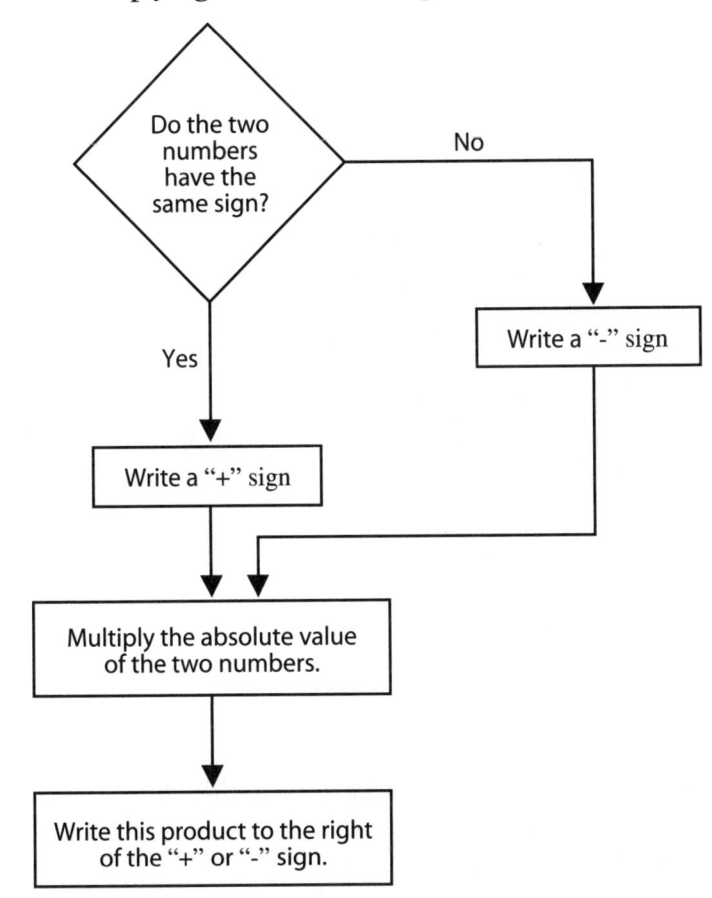

```
        ┌─────────────┐
       ╱ Do the two   ╲
      ╱  numbers       ╲────No────┐
      ╲  have the      ╱          │
       ╲ same sign?   ╱           ▼
        └─────────────┘      ┌──────────────┐
             │               │ Write a "−"  │
            Yes              │    sign      │
             ▼               └──────────────┘
      ┌──────────────┐              │
      │ Write a "+"  │              │
      │    sign      │              │
      └──────────────┘              │
             │                      │
             ▼◄─────────────────────┘
      ┌──────────────────────────┐
      │ Multiply the absolute    │
      │ value of the two numbers.│
      └──────────────────────────┘
             │
             ▼
      ┌──────────────────────────┐
      │ Write this product to the│
      │ right of the "+" or "−"  │
      │ sign.                    │
      └──────────────────────────┘
```

Chapter Five

Flowcharting can be as fun as child's play! But facilitating systemic thinking and real-world skill-building is a challenging and worthy endeavor. Think about it. Try it. You'll see!

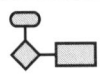

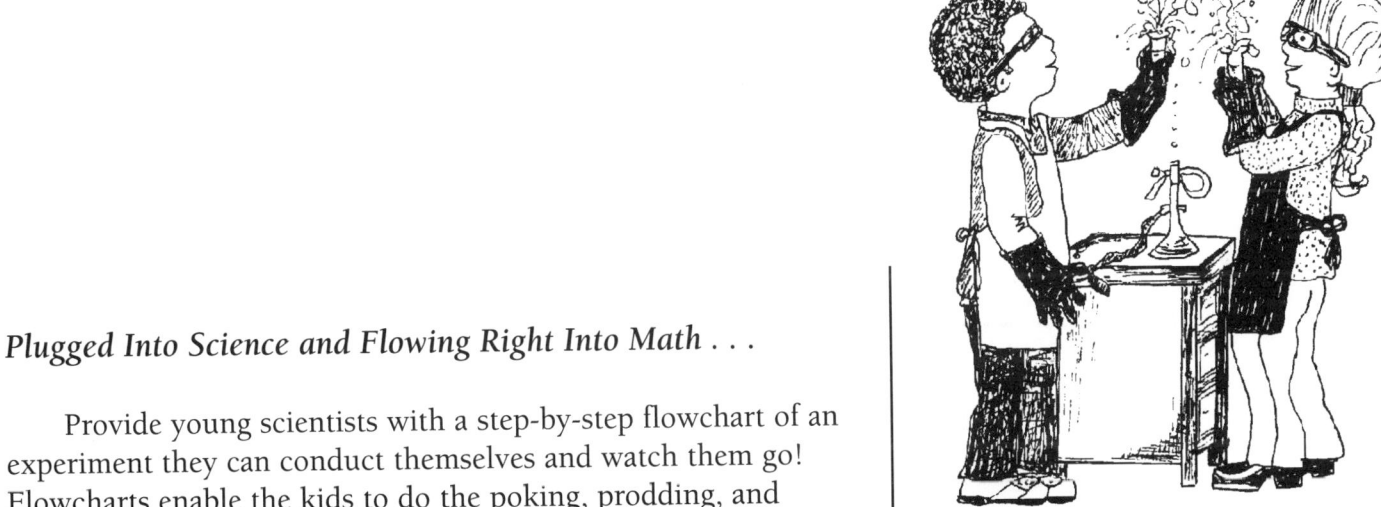

Plugged Into Science and Flowing Right Into Math . . .

Provide young scientists with a step-by-step flowchart of an experiment they can conduct themselves and watch them go! Flowcharts enable the kids to do the poking, prodding, and hypothesizing. In the first example, you will see a simple flowchart that guided young children as they tested and compared temperatures.

The second example looks a lot more complex, but this flowchart was used by itty-bitty scientists, too. This clever teacher provided the kids with a deployment flowchart that clarified roles, responsibilities, tasks, and decision points. To help these young ones follow along on a rather sophisticated journey, this teacher took care to make this into a huge, class-size flowchart and decorated it with Polaroid pictures of stakeholders, empty bags of candy, role hats, a bar graph complete with crayons—all stapled or glued to the corresponding position on the flowchart. A little thoughtfulness goes such a long way!

WHAT TEMPERATURE IS BEST?

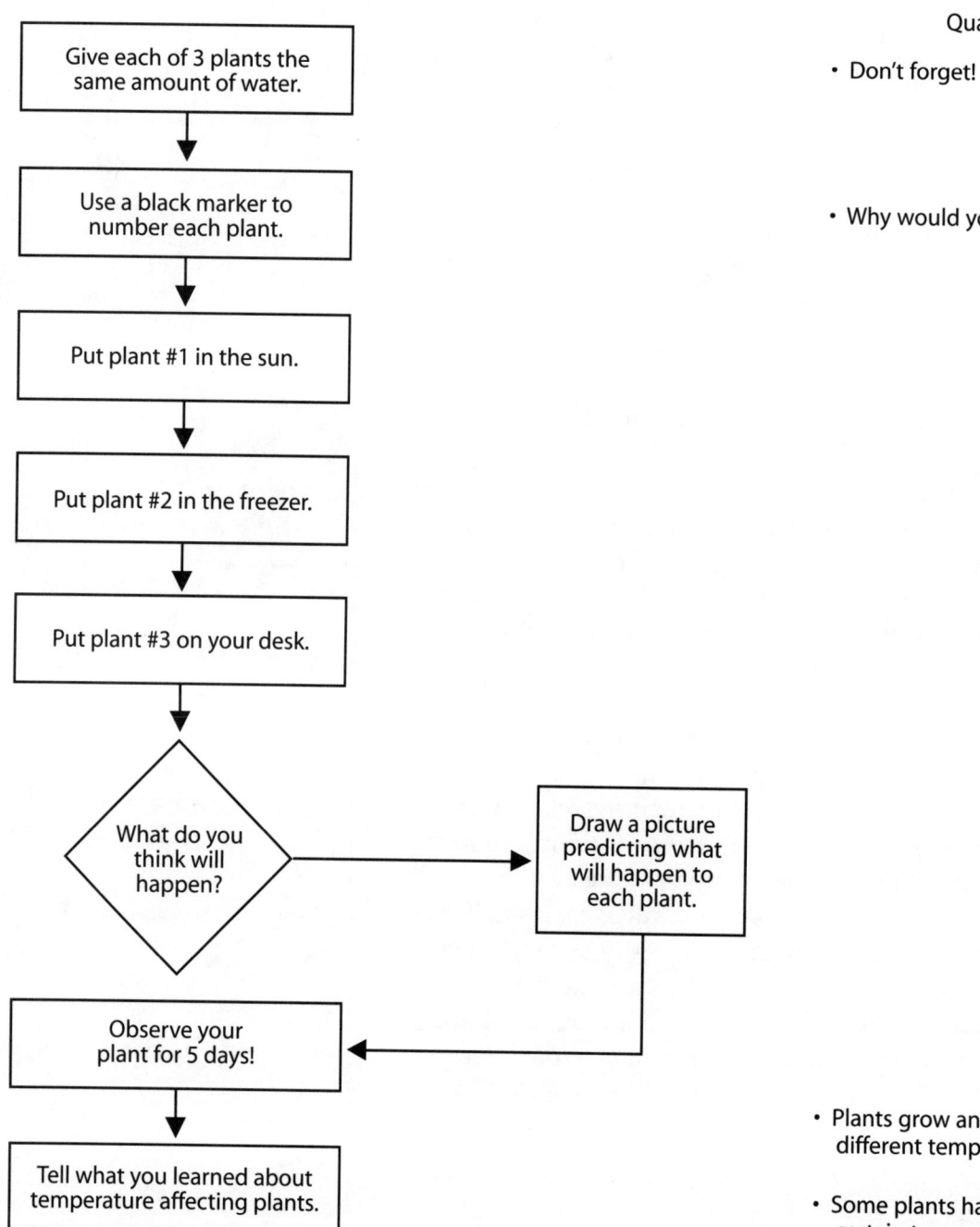

```
┌─────────────────────────────┐
│ Give each of 3 plants the   │
│    same amount of water.    │
└─────────────┬───────────────┘
              ▼
┌─────────────────────────────┐
│    Use a black marker to    │
│      number each plant.     │
└─────────────┬───────────────┘
              ▼
┌─────────────────────────────┐
│  Put plant #1 in the sun.   │
└─────────────┬───────────────┘
              ▼
┌─────────────────────────────┐
│ Put plant #2 in the freezer.│
└─────────────┬───────────────┘
              ▼
┌─────────────────────────────┐
│  Put plant #3 on your desk. │
└─────────────┬───────────────┘
              ▼
          ╱ What do ╲            ┌──────────────────┐
         ╱  you     ╲────────────▶│ Draw a picture   │
         ╲  think will╱            │ predicting what  │
          ╲ happen? ╱             │ will happen to   │
           ╲───────╱              │ each plant.      │
              │                   └─────────┬────────┘
              ▼                             │
┌─────────────────────────────┐             │
│      Observe your           │◀────────────┘
│    plant for 5 days!        │
└─────────────┬───────────────┘
              ▼
┌─────────────────────────────┐
│ Tell what you learned about │
│ temperature affecting plants│
└─────────────────────────────┘
```

Quality Issues

- Don't forget!

- Why would you mark each plant?

- Plants grow and survive in different temperatures.

- Some plants have to grow in certain temperatures to survive.

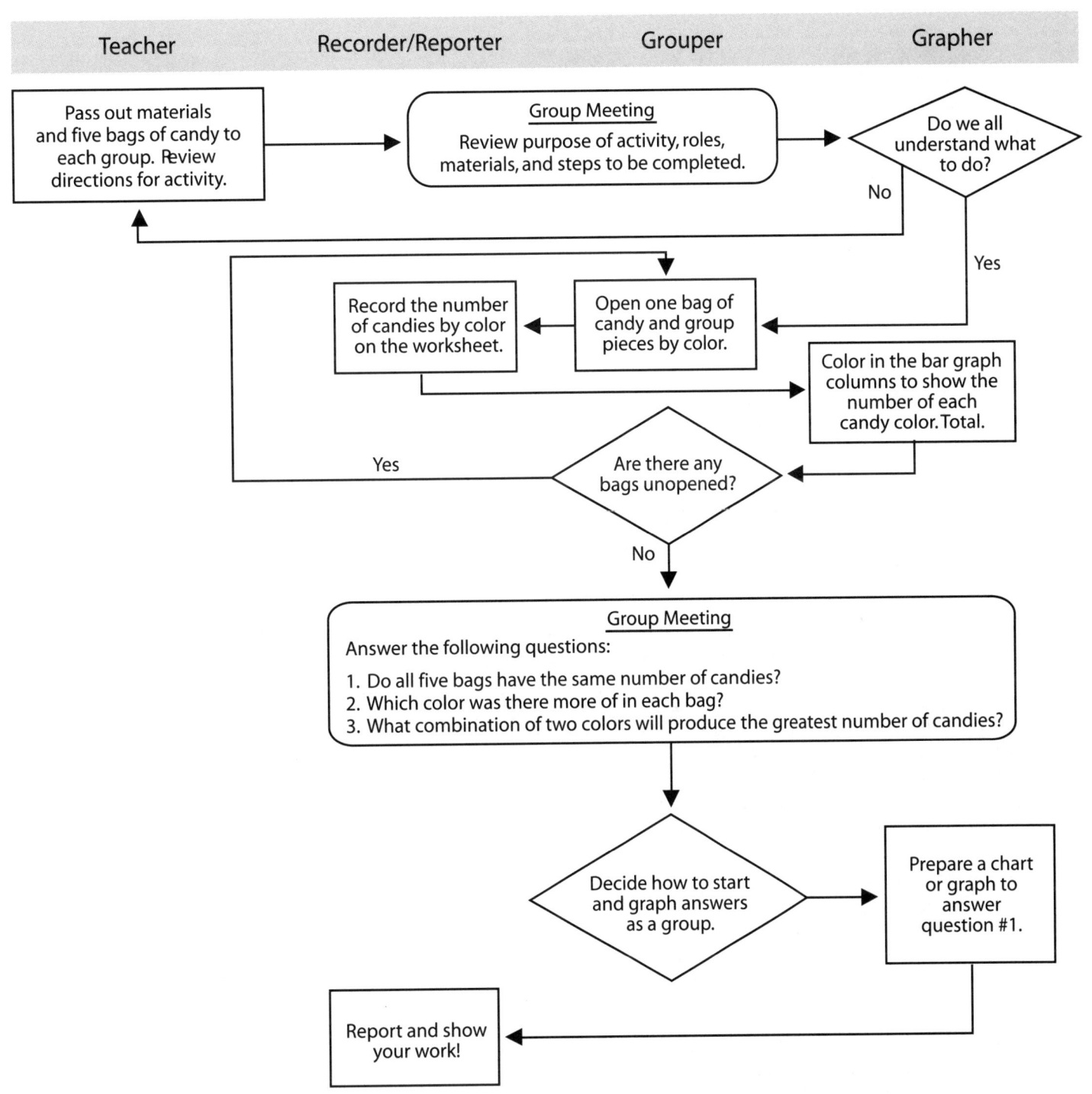

Flowchart

Teacher	Recorder/Reporter	Grouper	Grapher

Pass out materials and five bags of candy to each group. Review directions for activity.

→ **Group Meeting**: Review purpose of activity, roles, materials, and steps to be completed.

→ **Do we all understand what to do?**
- No → (back to Group Meeting)
- Yes ↓

Open one bag of candy and group pieces by color.

→ **Record the number of candies by color on the worksheet.**

→ **Color in the bar graph columns to show the number of each candy color. Total.**

→ **Are there any bags unopened?**
- Yes → (back to Open one bag of candy)
- No ↓

Group Meeting
Answer the following questions:
1. Do all five bags have the same number of candies?
2. Which color was there more of in each bag?
3. What combination of two colors will produce the greatest number of candies?

↓

Decide how to start and graph answers as a group.

→ **Prepare a chart or graph to answer question #1.**

→ **Report and show your work!**

121

Chapter Five

Law and Order

But that's still not the end of the story! Suppose the law is challenged in court on constitutional grounds? Then what happens?

For even greater understanding of this process, have students do a deployment flowchart describing the entire life of a bill beginning with its introduction in Congress.

Kids can examine how all the branches of government are involved in making and interpreting laws. They'll conclude that our founding fathers were pretty smart!

Hint: At the top of this flowchart, you can use a people coordinate to denote "Legislative, Executive, Judicial" branches as the people or bodies of people involved.

Plugging Into Social Studies

So when Congress passes a bill, it becomes a law. Right? Not necessarily! The following flowchart helped these students track the steps as the bill left Congress and moved through the process.

This flowchart demonstrates that narrative is not always the clearest communication vehicle. Can you see how a process comes to life right before your eyes? Yes, this is how a flowchart helps to create process thinking!

LAW AND ORDER

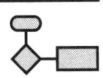

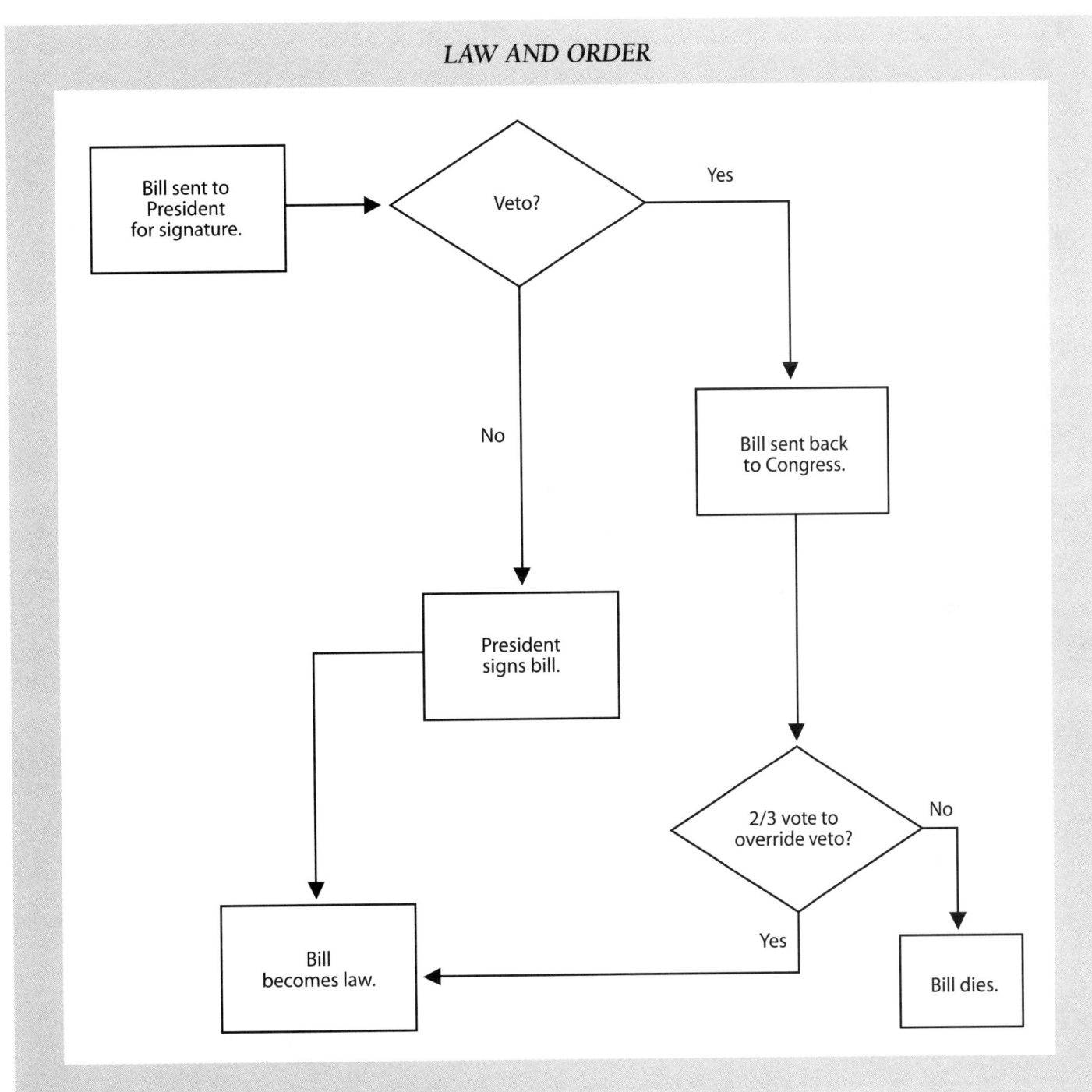

- Bill sent to President for signature. → **Veto?**
  - No → President signs bill. → Bill becomes law.
  - Yes → Bill sent back to Congress. → **2/3 vote to override veto?**
    - Yes → Bill becomes law.
    - No → Bill dies.

Chapter Five

Plugged Into Safety

So, what do you do when that storm comes up suddenly? It all depends on where you are at the time. This flowchart makes it clear! Storms, earthquakes, fires, and floods are natural ways Mother Nature reminds us of our systemic universe. Flowcharting processes to adapt is a practical and effective approach towards preparedness.

Preparing for safe steps and decisions is an important mind-set to develop. Have your class brainstorm potential safety threats in their lives. Then break them into teams to flowchart plans that will help them anticipate and prepare for wise action in a quality way.

What if a stranger wants to talk to me? What if I come home to an empty house? Fire? A party where someone might drink, then drive?! All of these are real issues for real kids in real life. Flowcharting is a real tool that really works.

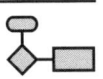

STORMY WEATHER

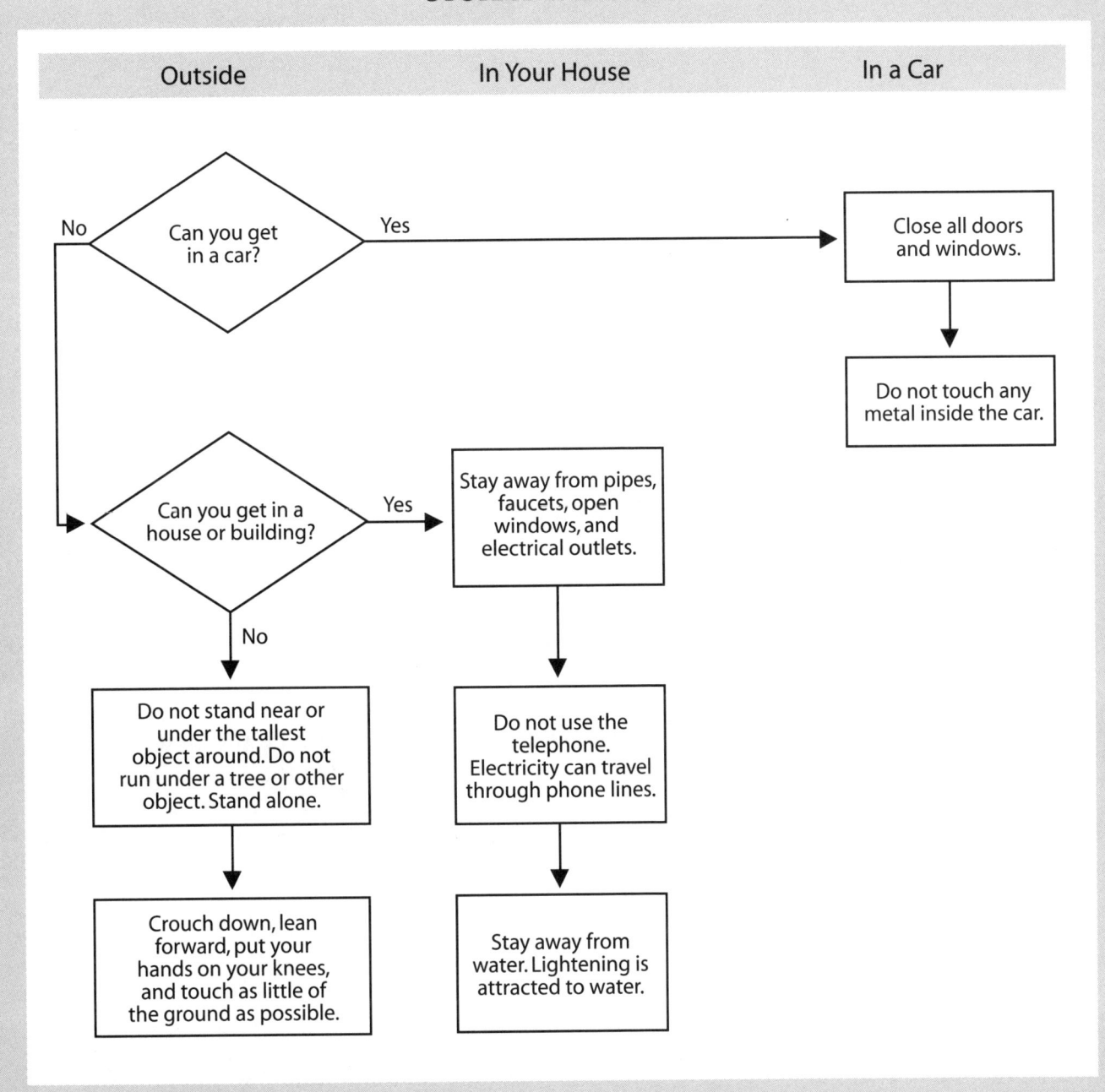

Outside

Can you get in a car?

- **Yes** → Close all doors and windows. → Do not touch any metal inside the car.
- **No** → Can you get in a house or building?
  - **Yes** → Stay away from pipes, faucets, open windows, and electrical outlets. → Do not use the telephone. Electricity can travel through phone lines. → Stay away from water. Lightening is attracted to water.
  - **No** → Do not stand near or under the tallest object around. Do not run under a tree or other object. Stand alone. → Crouch down, lean forward, put your hands on your knees, and touch as little of the ground as possible.

Chapter Five

Plugging Into Literature

Whether you're teaching the kids to listen for basic elements of a story or having students foreshadow the outcome, the flowchart is a powerful learning adventure. Younger kids can flowchart the basic elements as they become more focused listeners, more focused readers. Older students can identify decision points in the story, imagine the thought processes and dilemmas encountered during those decision points, and then try to determine what criteria was used in making the decision that took the character/story in the direction that unfolds. As with main characters, they can even do this in regards to the author. They can put themselves in the author's mind and then try to determine why the author chose to go this way or that—what literary power was brought to the story by the author's decisions.

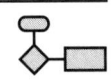

Flowchart

TAKING NOTES ON A STORY

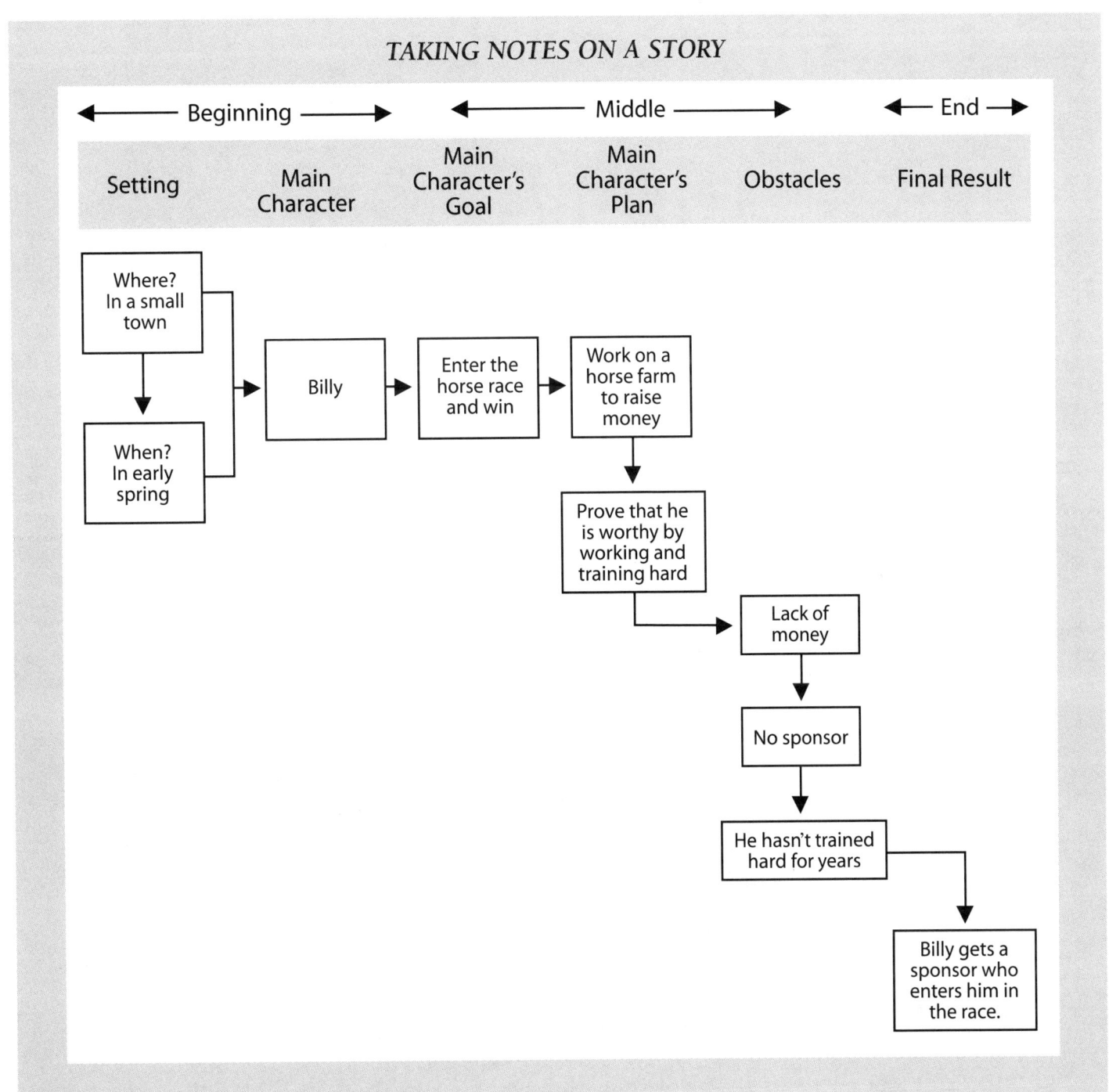

← Beginning →	← Middle →	← End →
Setting · Main Character	Main Character's Goal · Main Character's Plan · Obstacles	Final Result

- Where? In a small town
- When? In early spring

→ Billy → Enter the horse race and win → Work on a horse farm to raise money → Prove that he is worthy by working and training hard → Lack of money → No sponsor → He hasn't trained hard for years → Billy gets a sponsor who enters him in the race.

127

Chapter Five

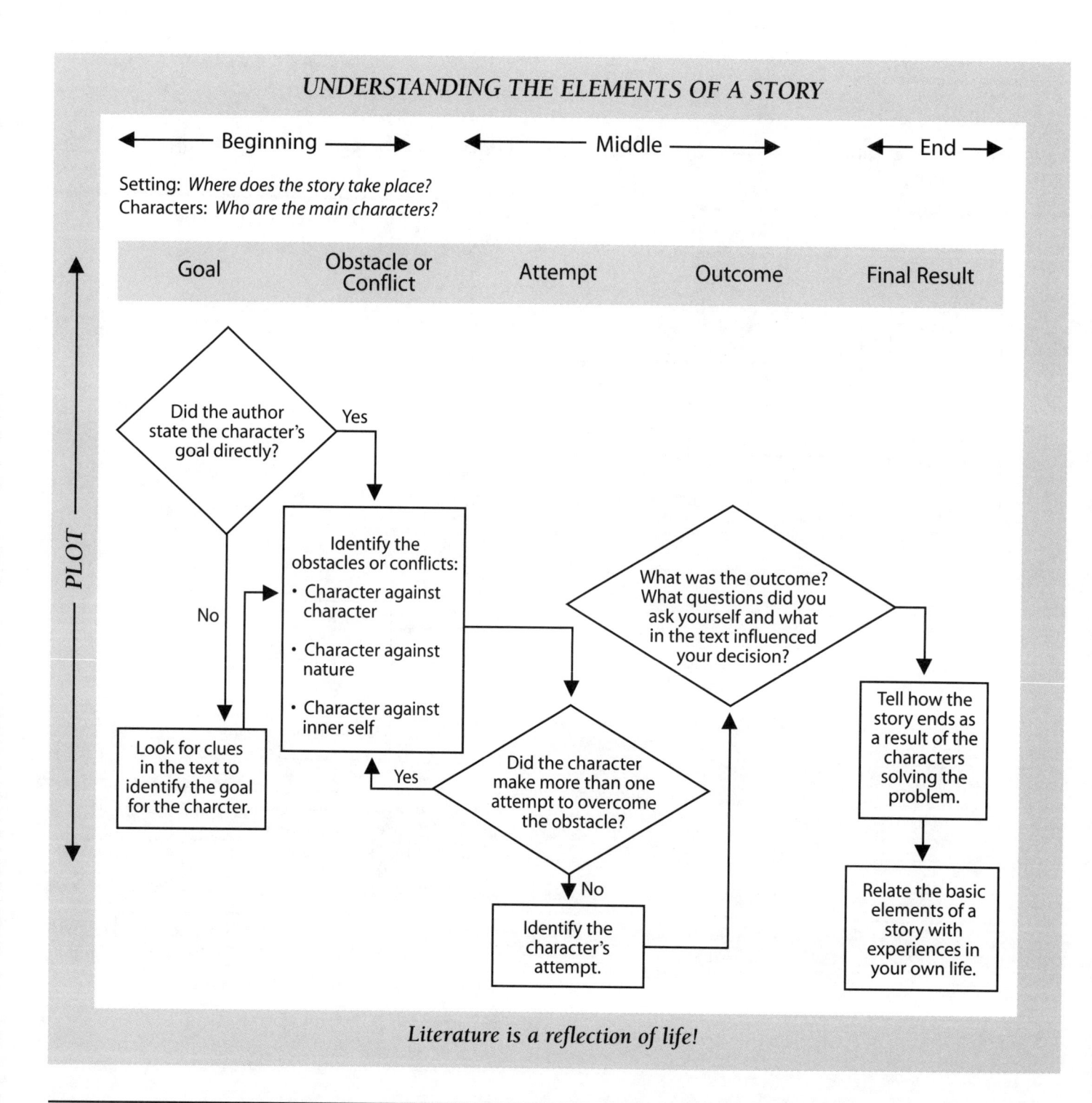

UNDERSTANDING THE ELEMENTS OF A STORY

◄— Beginning —► ◄— Middle —► ◄— End —►

Setting: *Where does the story take place?*
Characters: *Who are the main characters?*

PLOT

| Goal | Obstacle or Conflict | Attempt | Outcome | Final Result |

Did the author state the character's goal directly?
- Yes → Identify the obstacles or conflicts:
  - Character against character
  - Character against nature
  - Character against inner self
- No → Look for clues in the text to identify the goal for the character.

Did the character make more than one attempt to overcome the obstacle?
- Yes → (back to obstacles)
- No → Identify the character's attempt.

What was the outcome? What questions did you ask yourself and what in the text influenced your decision?

Tell how the story ends as a result of the characters solving the problem.

Relate the basic elements of a story with experiences in your own life.

Literature is a reflection of life!

128

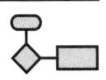

IDENTIFYING MOOD IN A STORY

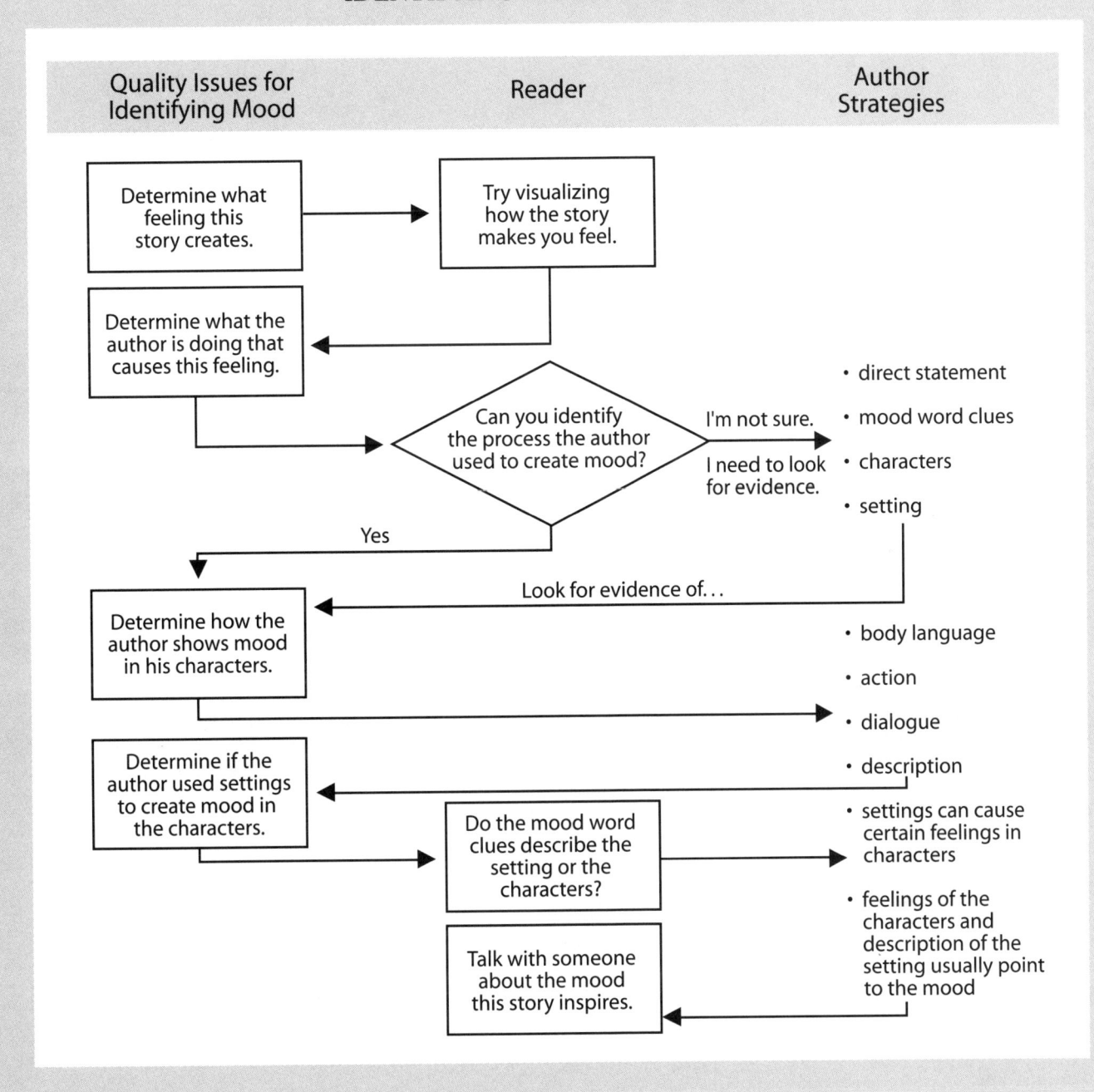

Quality Issues for Identifying Mood	Reader	Author Strategies
Determine what feeling this story creates.	Try visualizing how the story makes you feel.	
Determine what the author is doing that causes this feeling.		

Can you identify the process the author used to create mood?

- I'm not sure.
- I need to look for evidence.

- direct statement
- mood word clues
- characters
- setting

Yes

Look for evidence of…

Determine how the author shows mood in his characters.

- body language
- action
- dialogue
- description

Determine if the author used settings to create mood in the characters.

Do the mood word clues describe the setting or the characters?

- settings can cause certain feelings in characters
- feelings of the characters and description of the setting usually point to the mood

Talk with someone about the mood this story inspires.

Chapter Five

Three Before Me?

To encourage students to develop the important skill of working independently, many teachers try the "Three Before Me" rule. In a class where the "Three Before Me" rule is at work, here is what happens when a teacher responds to a raised hand.

1. The student shows the teacher where he has tried to find the information in the textbook or notes.

2. The student tells the teacher the name of a student he has consulted to try to find the answer or missing information.

3. The student tells the teacher the name of a second student he has consulted to try to find the answer or missing information.

Hint: The teacher addresses all three students and provides the needed help—while at the same time encouraging autonomy!

Plugged Into Classroom Management . . .

Some teachers (not you) have said, "My kids always come in saying, 'What are we going to do today?'" Have your students ever asked you that question? With the flowchart, they'll never have to ask again—they'll know!

Use a deployment flowchart to plan with your kids. Then post it on the board or on the wall. Everyone—even visitors—can see the flow of the class.

It's so easy . . . why haven't we always done it this way?

Flowchart

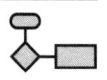

WHAT'S UP?

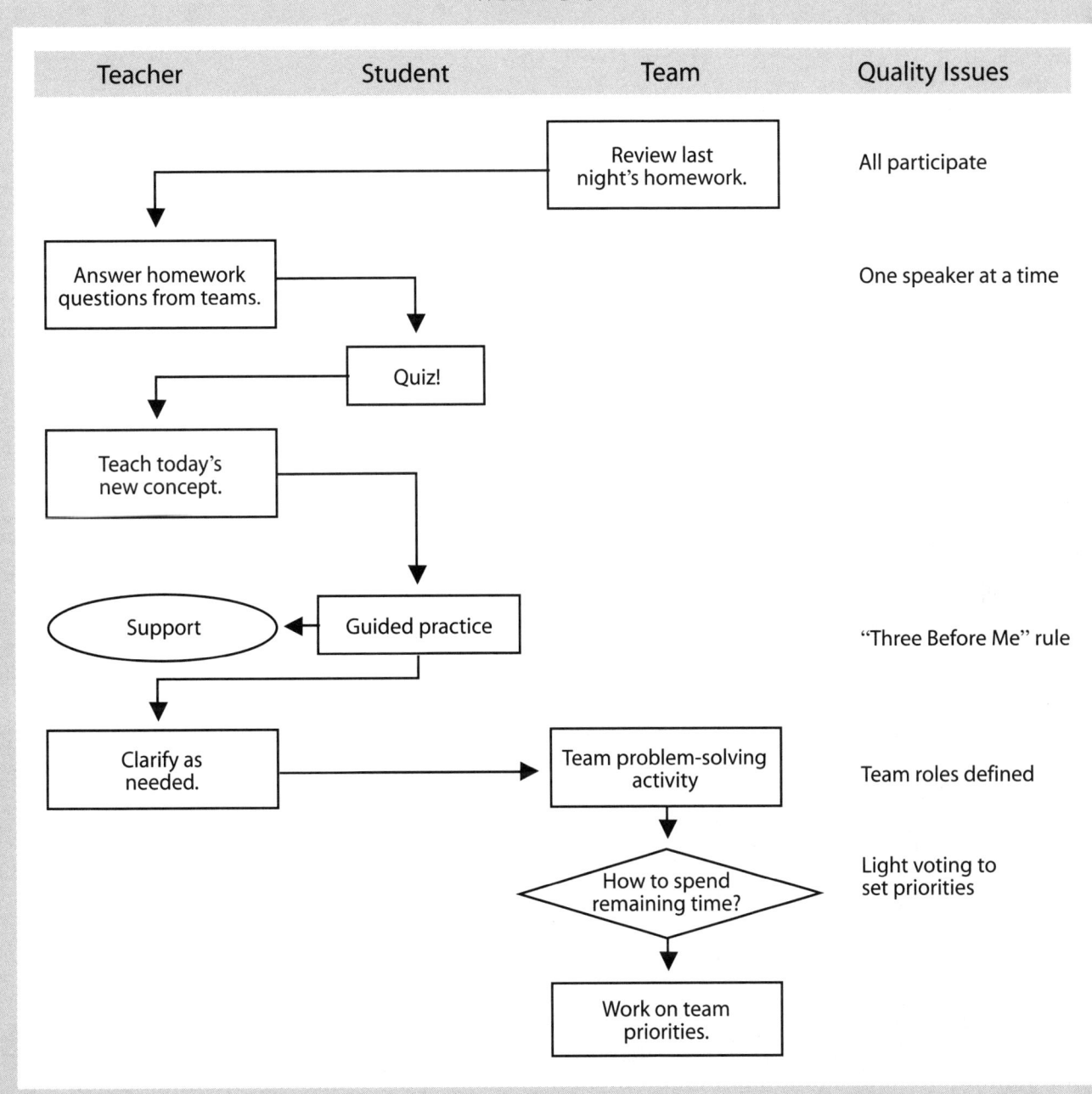

Teacher	Student	Team	Quality Issues
		Review last night's homework.	All participate
Answer homework questions from teams.			One speaker at a time
	Quiz!		
Teach today's new concept.			
Support ← Guided practice			"Three Before Me" rule
Clarify as needed.		Team problem-solving activity	Team roles defined
		How to spend remaining time?	Light voting to set priorities
		Work on team priorities.	

Chapter Five

CURRICULUM IDEAS FROM A TO Z

LANGUAGE ARTS

- Steps in determining how to sequence or summarize a story
- Events leading up to the climax or turning point of a story
- Steps in researching, writing, and/or improving a research paper
- The creation of a friendly or business letter

SOCIAL STUDIES

- Events in a battle
- The election process
- Events leading up to a war
- The judicial appeals process
- A country's evolution from economic dependency to an independent economy
- How political officials are elected
- How laws are created and passed
- Migration of immigrants to the U.S. from various countries
- How third world countries select leaders

SCIENCE

- The layering of sediments
- Circuits: How to light two bulbs with one cell
- How clouds form
- How acid rain is formed
- How the Gulf Stream helps keep the East Coast warm
- What NASA has learned from its unmanned probes in the past 30 years
- The mitosis or meiosis process
- Life cycle of animals
- Chemical reactions in an experiment
- Formation of a hurricane

HEALTH & P.E.

- Rules of a game or event
- Procedures for administering a type of first aid
- Good sportsmanship practices
- Analysis of an athletic performance or event
- A healthy day's diet based on the food pyramid
- Evolution of specific types of dances in various cultures

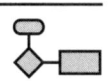

CURRICULUM IDEAS FROM A TO Z

VOCATIONAL

- Diagnosing a car that won't start
- Computer procedures
- Safety procedures when cooking
- Using a recipe

GUIDANCE

- Steps in the college application process
- Developing a four-year plan for high school
- Determining eligibility for college scholarships

MATH

- Graphing an equation using the slope and y-intercept
- Determining the shape of a quadratic equation's graph
- Identifying a geometric shape by its characteristics
- Solving an equation
- Order of operations in simplifying expressions
- Long division
- Any problem-solving process

ARTS & DANCE

- Choreography
- Movement in a scene in a dramatic production
- Evolution of specific types of dances in various cultures
- Steps in making papier-mâché mask
- Process for making a ceramic vase
- Evolution of painting techniques

Chapter Five

NOTES

Flowchart

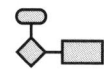

NOTES

DOG
Live in doghouse...
Eat dog food
Live inside house...
Eat steak!

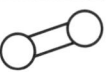

CHAPTER SIX

BONE DIAGRAM

Why Use a Bone Diagram to Uncover My Curriculum?

To effectively uncover the curriculum, you and your students will have to identify and articulate the current state, envision the desired future state, and analyze the gap between here and there . . . and then, of course, identify goals to achieve, tasks to reach your goals, the driving forces that will help you get there, and the restraining forces that may impede progress. Being the quality thinkers that you are, of course, you will also build in an ongoing assessment process that allows you to continuously assess your progress and identify opportunities for improvement. Quite a process—a *process* that focuses on the *process* and leads to results!

Can a bone diagram do all that all by itself? Not really, other quality tools will come into play; however, the bone diagram is a tool that helps students visualize and document this strategic planning process from start to finish. "Begin with the end in mind." And, if you're going to begin with the end in mind, you're gonna have to figure out where you're currently at, don't you think? The bone diagram will help you and your students do just that!

> **CHALLENGE**
>
> "Begin with the end in mind" is one of the seven habits of highly effective people. Who is the wise man who coined this phrase and in what book?

> **CHALLENGE**
>
> - What is Hoshin Planning?
> - How does strategic planning fit into Total Quality?
> - Why would you use strategic planning?
> - How do you build student-teacher partnerships?
> - Who pioneered the concept of classroom learning systems?

Chapter Six

It looks like a dog bone and is as user-friendly as a dog bone. In its simplicity, it processes complexity. Students of all ages enjoy chewin' on this bone!

This tool will not only help you and your students prepare to uncover your curriculum in a quality way, but as you will see as you browse through the examples created in real, live classrooms, the bone diagram helps to uncover specific curriculum content—applying the current state/future state mind journey in a host of subject areas.

Bone

How Do I Use a Bone Diagram to Uncover the Curriculum?

Process

1. Introduce the topic, identifying purpose, goals, and desired outcomes. With your class, discuss how this topic fits into the big picture—this particular course or grade, other course and grade requirements . . . the real world.

2. Introduce the bone diagram as a tool that identifies current state and future state, or identifies a beginning state and end state, identifies the gap or transition space, events, actions, or goals, as well as the driving and restraining forces. Explain that this tool can be used to plan and improve the learning process, or to investigate curriculum content.

3. Begin with a drawing like this:

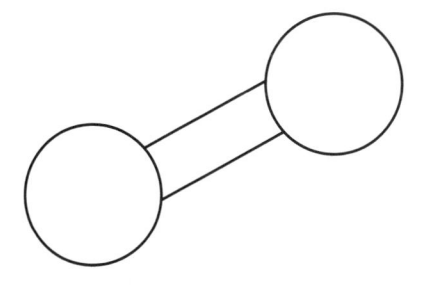

4. Label the first part of the bone "present state" and the other end of the bone "future state."

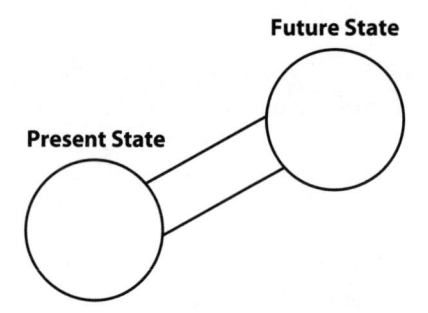

Present State

Future State

5. Have students identify conditions and/or realities that currently exist. For example, if you were an early elementary teacher looking at the writing process, your bone might look something like this:

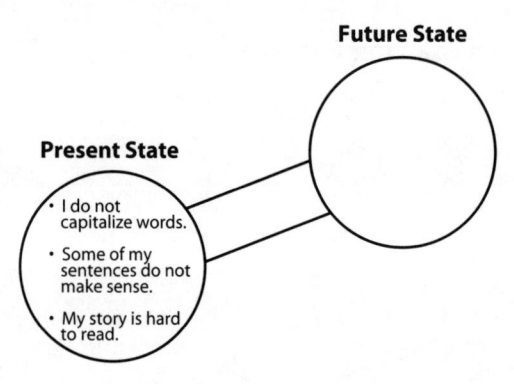

Present State
- I do not capitalize words.
- Some of my sentences do not make sense.
- My story is hard to read.

Future State

Bone

6. Have students envision what their work will look like in the future after they have reached the objectives of the writing curriculum at this grade level.

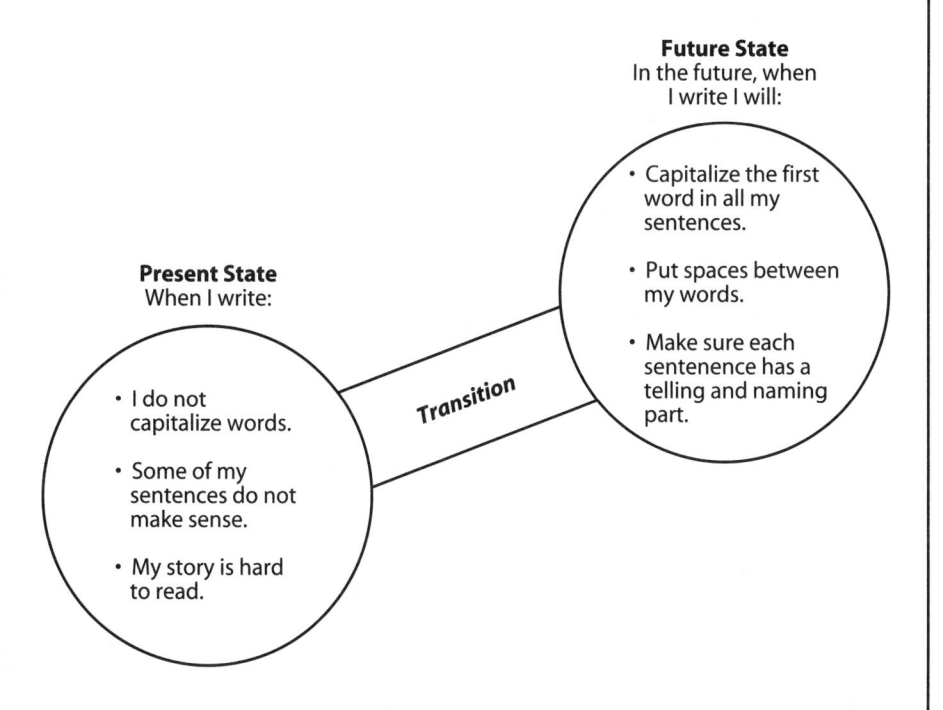

Present State
When I write:

- I do not capitalize words.
- Some of my sentenences do not make sense.
- My story is hard to read.

Transition

Future State
In the future, when I write I will:

- Capitalize the first word in all my sentences.
- Put spaces between my words.
- Make sure each sentenence has a telling and naming part.

Don't Worry . . .
Be Happy!

There are lots of ways to do this . . .

- Current State and Future State
- Beginning and Ending
- Before and After

You figure it out!

Chapter Six

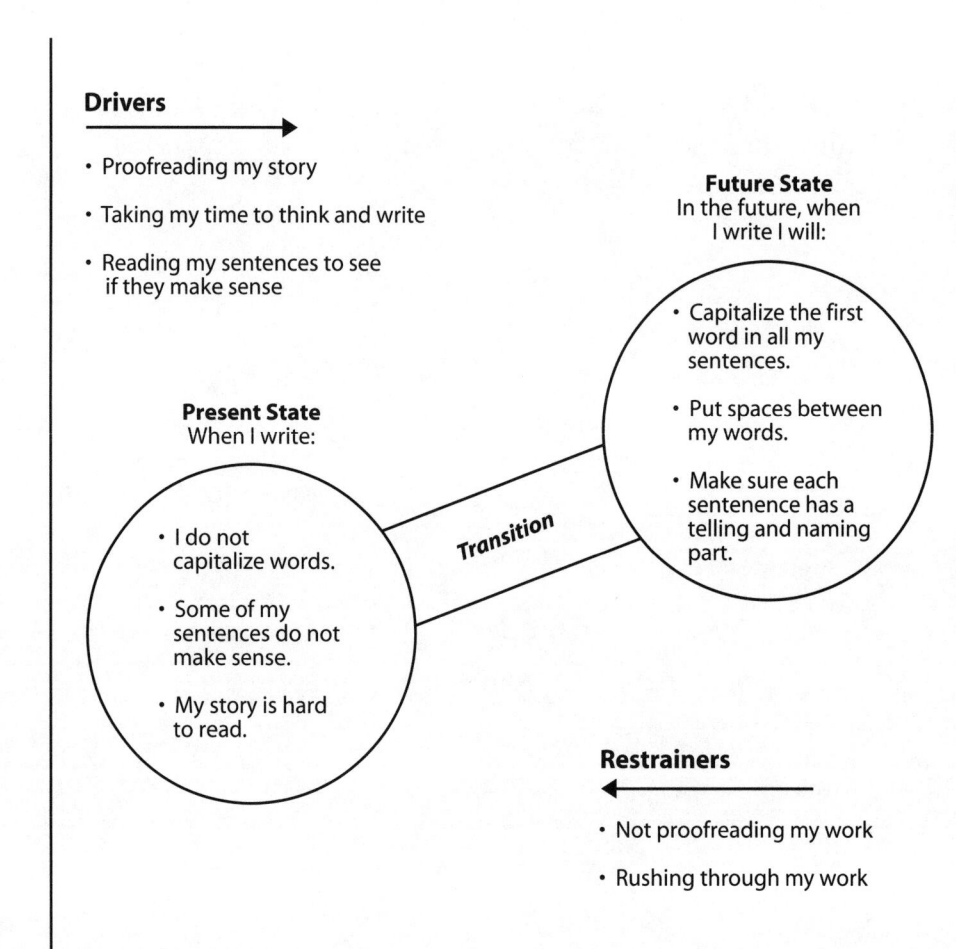

Drivers →

- Proofreading my story
- Taking my time to think and write
- Reading my sentences to see if they make sense

Present State
When I write:

- I do not capitalize words.
- Some of my sentences do not make sense.
- My story is hard to read.

Transition

Future State
In the future, when I write I will:

- Capitalize the first word in all my sentences.
- Put spaces between my words.
- Make sure each sentence has a telling and naming part.

Restrainers ←

- Not proofreading my work
- Rushing through my work

7. Have students identify drivers and restrainers. Hint: In actuality you will be using the force field process. With younger students, you can usually capture the drivers and restrainers on the same sheet, whereas with older students and more complex tasks/issues, a force field diagram can be constructed separately.

8. Engage in dialogue with your students. Ask questions such as:

    - "Why did we do this?"

    - "What have we learned?"

    - "What is the power of this process?"

9. Discuss next steps, identify goals, tasks, and timelines. Create an action plan.

Chapter Six

Plugged Into Social Studies, Civics, and Economics?

The bone diagram can be used to examine the current state of affairs and then to envision the future state of civic events, economic policy, foreign policy, and the like. Using this process is an effective way to expose students at any grade level to world events. They will learn to clarify current situations, anticipate potential outcomes, and analyze contributing and competing forces.

The bone diagram is also a great way to examine historical events. The following example demonstrates how one classroom of high school students used the bone diagram to follow the early American patriots' pathway to independence, first by identifying a start point in time, and then identifying a significant end point or hallmark in history. Investigating the conditions, events, and beliefs came to life as these high schoolers conceptualized the driving and restraining forces encountered by our revolutionary forefathers.

Drivers →

- Representation in government
- Wealthy merchants
- Trade possibilities
- Economic benefit
- Taxation without representation

U.S. Before American Revolution

- Colonial Assembly
- Parliament governed
- Royal governors
- No representation
- King George III
- No established military
- Colonial military—British army

Transition

U.S. After American Revolution

- Weak central government
- Articles of Confederation
- Strong state governments
- Confederation Congress
- No real executive
- Small standing army
- State militias
- States controlled own affairs—like 13 countries

Restrainers ←

- Lack of navy
- Loyalty to king
- Fear of failure
- Fear of the unknown

Chapter Six

Plugged Into Science . . . A Definite Fit!

The concepts of current state and future state take on a whole new flavor when you take the bone diagram into the laboratory! In the following example, elementary students were studying mixtures and solutions. These very young scientists were tasked to conduct an experiment to see if mixtures can be separated—using the bone diagram to get the mix of things.

After labeling the top of the bones "current state," these kids chose sand and salt as their mixture of choice. They wrote their hypothesis in the bone labeled "future state." Then they identified the steps of the experiment as the drivers and the events or conditions that do not allow separation as the restrainers.

Bone

Drivers (What will drive
the mixture to separate?)
→

- Pouring water on the mixture
- Filtering sand through a sieve
- Letting the water evaporate

Present State

The sand and salt are mixed together in a container.

Transition—The Experiment

Future State

The sand and salt are separated.

Restrainers (What will not
allow the mixture to separate?)
←

- Using a chemical solution

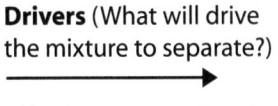

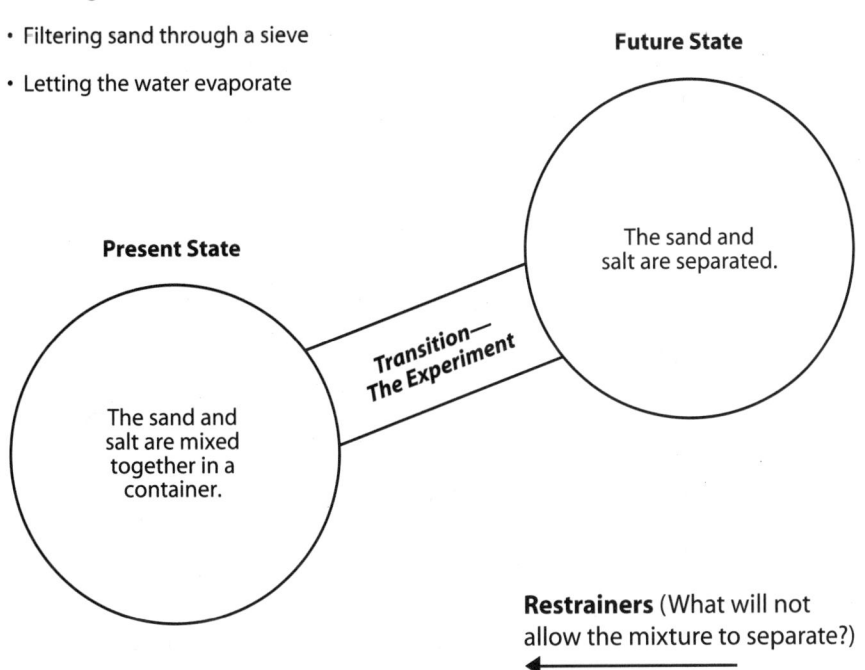

Don't you think this bone lends itself to the scientific method?

Can Kids Plug Into Spiraling Curriculum?

Kids need to acquire an understanding of the spiraling curriculum process. After all, it's their curriculum, too! Not only does the bone diagram help kids embrace the spiraling curriculum with a clear understanding of how getting from current state to the projected future state requires goals, plans, and continuous assessment, but also helps them to co-create shared accountability. The kids learn to anticipate their future, begin the learning process with the end in mind. They learn to become the active players in the classroom working with you to uncover the curriculum.

Bone

Drivers →

- Listen in class
- Read 15 minutes every night
- Complete all our work
- Do our homework
- Practice at home with parents

Present State (2nd Grade)

- We learned addition facts
- We learned our subtraction facts
- We learned to read fairy tales
- We learned how to take care of plants

Transition

Future State (3rd Grade)

- We will learn about multiplication facts
- We will learn how to divide
- We will learn about animals and where they live
- We will learn about keeping safe
- We will learn to read chapter books

Restrainers ←

- Not listening in class
- Playing instead of doing our work
- Not reading at home
- Coming to school unprepared

Chapter Six

Bones Plugged Into Literature

Much like the bone diagram can be used to examine historical events, it can be used to uncover literature at every grade level. In the following example, young students used the bone diagram to compare the opening situation with the final scene. Yes, of course, they had serious dialogue about what drove the characters to resolution as well as the obstacles they encountered along the way.

Drivers ("drove" the resolution)

- Carly tried to make her grandfather laugh by making him secret gifts
- Carly's grandfather made Carly a cornhusk doll for her birthday
- Carly learned to enjoy working on the farm

Future State (end of story)

- Carly loved her grandfather and enjoyed living with him on the farm
- Carly's grandfather smiled and laughed more!

Present State (beginning of story)

- Carly had to go live with her elderly grandfather while her parents were gone for a year.
- Carly didn't want to go.
- Grandfather was stern.

Transition

Restrainers (obstacles or events along the way)

- Carly had never met her grandfather
- Carly lived in the city and her grandfather lived on a farm
- Carly's grandfather did not laugh or smile
- Carly's grandather did not know how to deal with children

151

Chapter Six

Plugged Into Health Science

Health science is specified and mandated educational curriculum. Health is a real-life issue that can be supported and even facilitated by caring loved ones and trained professionals. Commitment to a healthy lifestyle is a real-life issue that can only be confronted and successfully embraced by each individual; however, guidance from an educated teacher can help.

So again, we are challenging you as teachers to help kids make the connections between classroom learning and real-life lessons.

A bone diagram is an energizing alternative to "telling" your young ones the facts and processes that lead to health and well-being. You can lead your kids through a process of "live" learning. Have your students use the bone diagram to identify and clarify current state for them as individuals at this point in time. Have them envision (with all senses) what health will look and feel like in the future state. Facilitate the process of identifying forces that drive good health, forces that restrain and thwart robust vigor and vim. Then support each and every young life within your realm of influence with sincerity and positive role modeling. Strengthen this stance by using tools and strategies that actively engage them to trigger awareness and pursue the knowledge necessary to foster values and practices that lead to health and well-being.

And, while you're moving your young students to pursue healthy life habits and beliefs, you just might get swept up in those energizing and health vibes. Perhaps you will learn as much as your students. What a happy thought! Wouldn't that be shared learning at its finest!

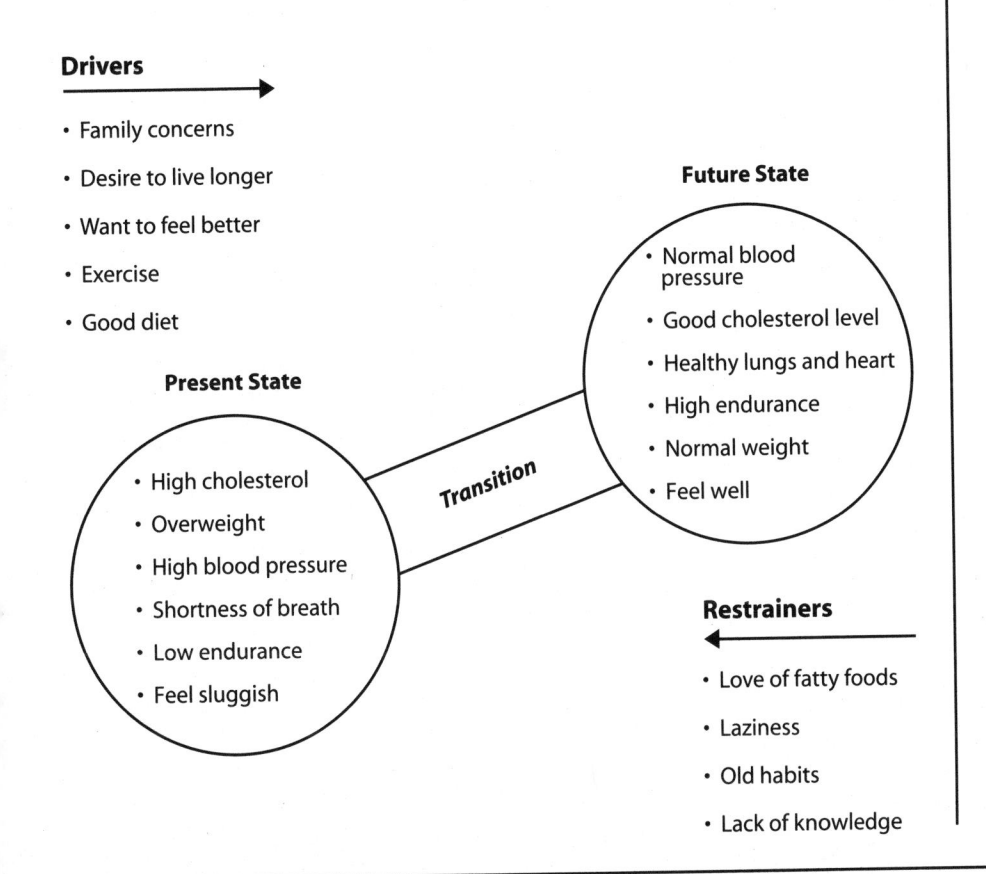

Drivers →

- Family concerns
- Desire to live longer
- Want to feel better
- Exercise
- Good diet

Present State

- High cholesterol
- Overweight
- High blood pressure
- Shortness of breath
- Low endurance
- Feel sluggish

Transition

Future State

- Normal blood pressure
- Good cholesterol level
- Healthy lungs and heart
- High endurance
- Normal weight
- Feel well

Restrainers ←

- Love of fatty foods
- Laziness
- Old habits
- Lack of knowledge

Plugged Into Classroom Democracy

Yes, classrooms are democracies, too. A democracy implies rights and responsibilities, shared ownership and accountability . . . a shared vision for success. So, to break that down into the bare bones of why, what, and how . . . turn the kids loose with the bone diagram, moral support, and wise guidance, and then watch them go! Democracy is the most powerful form of government—we know this from our own life experience, as well as from our respect for the insight and inspiration of the early Romans. How did they know the power of democracy so very long ago? Go wonder. Let's just do our part to keep the good times going . . . help our youngsters experience the rights and responsibilities of a stakeholder in a democratic system. In the following example you can see how this process begins with the very young.

Taking Care of Our Classroom—Everyone's Responsibility

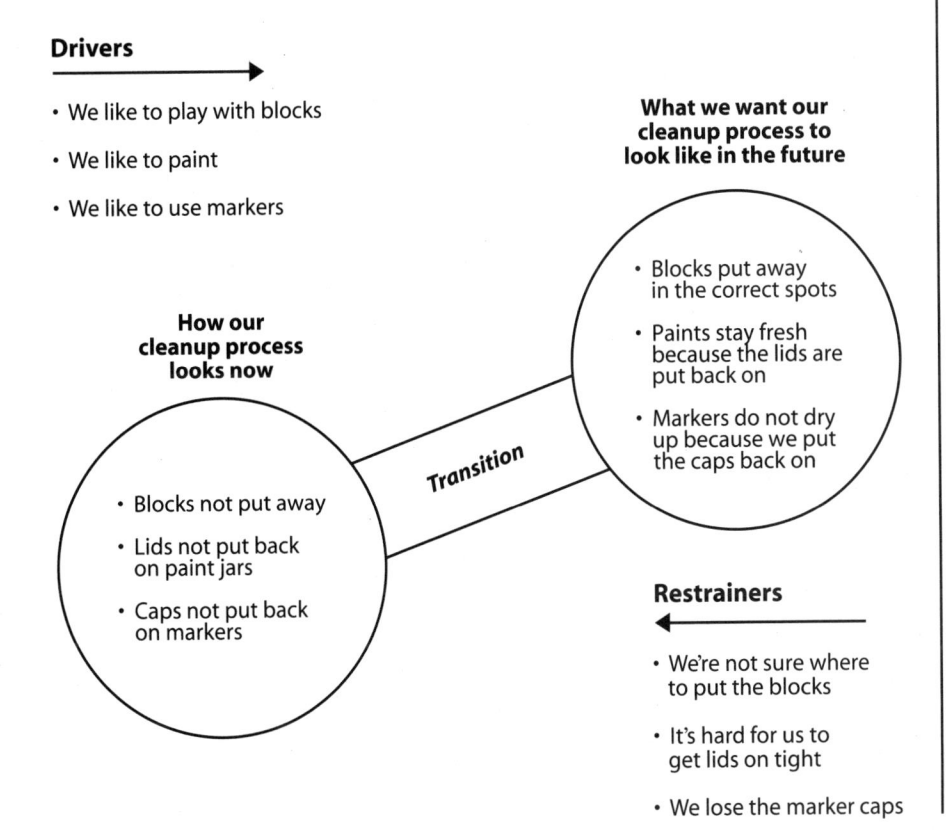

Drivers →

- We like to play with blocks
- We like to paint
- We like to use markers

How our cleanup process looks now

- Blocks not put away
- Lids not put back on paint jars
- Caps not put back on markers

Transition

What we want our cleanup process to look like in the future

- Blocks put away in the correct spots
- Paints stay fresh because the lids are put back on
- Markers do not dry up because we put the caps back on

Restrainers ←

- We're not sure where to put the blocks
- It's hard for us to get lids on tight
- We lose the marker caps

Working Together

These kids and their teacher identified opportunities for improvement, and then created a plan to make things happen.

OUR ACTION PLAN

1. Put pictures of correct blocks on shelves

2. Don't take the lid off. Punch holes in the top of the lids for brushes to fit through.

3. Assign a class supply keeper for pencils and markers.

Chapter Six

Parents Plugged In . . . Oh Yeah!

Parents are gonna want to be plugged in! When they start experiencing their children as key stakeholders and "movers and shakers" in their own learning journey, they're going to want to be invited in, encouraged, welcomed, and mentored through the process with effective tools and strategies.

Although in the initial stages, parents may balk with thoughts of "don't know how," "can't possibly," and "why are we changing, why are we breaking new ground?" They will all at once experience feelings of challenge, a wee bit of fear, skepticism, and believe it or not, a deep down desire of "wish I could, wish I could," followed by thoughts of "perhaps I can, perhaps I can" to the beginnings of "I think I can, I think I can." So, what's your job? To facilitate the process using tools and strategies that lead to verbalizations of, "I knew we could, I knew we could."

Up to the challenge? Of course you are!

The following example was created during a student-led conference by a powerful team—the student, teacher, and parent!

Drivers →

- College requirements
- Desire to please parents
- Wants a good job as an adult

Current Problems

- Low test scores
- Does not do homework
- Often absent
- Sleeps in class
- Does not participate in class discussion

Transition

Desired Future State

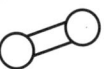

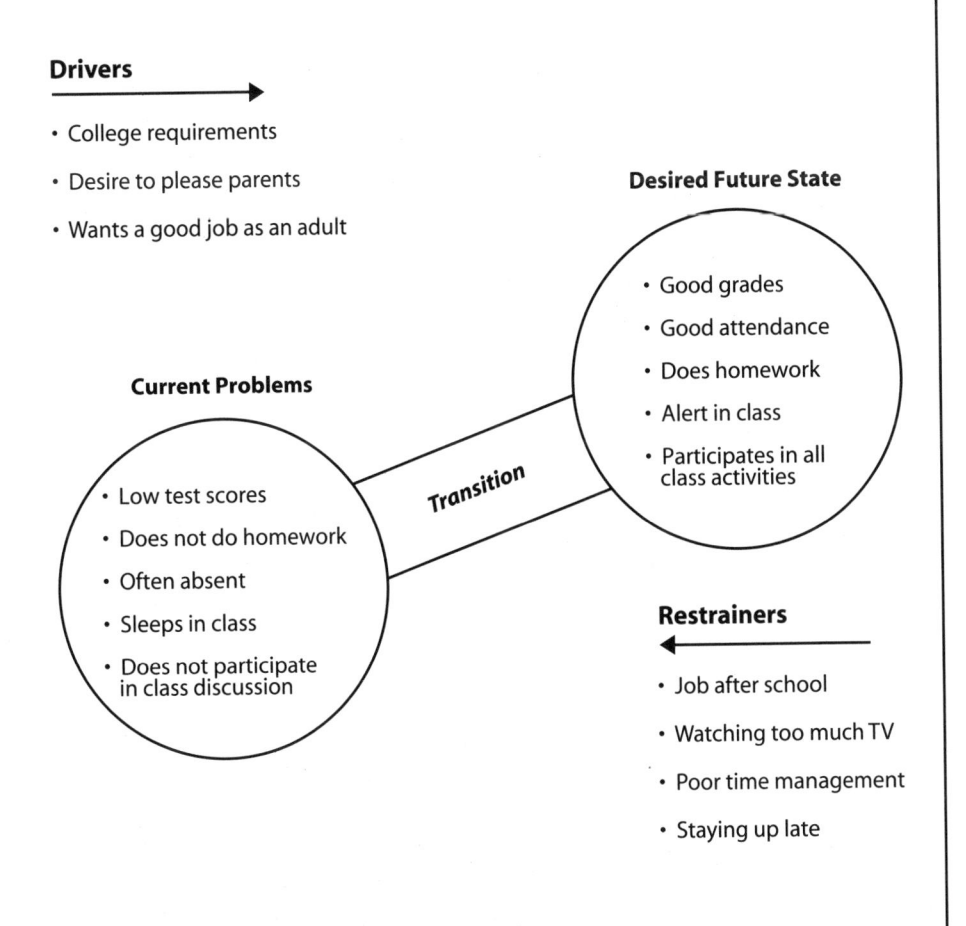

- Good grades
- Good attendance
- Does homework
- Alert in class
- Participates in all class activities

← **Restrainers**

- Job after school
- Watching too much TV
- Poor time management
- Staying up late

But don't stop here! Remember to create an action plan!

Chapter Six

Plugged Into Real-World Lessons for Real Live Kids

Sometimes we want to believe that childhood, adolescence, and young adulthood are carefree, filled with adventure and fun. True enough. However, in reality, kids in all these age groups face day-to-day experiences that are challenging and often escalate into problems that feel overwhelming. Is it your job to figure out the solution, solve the problem? No. Double no. But it is your job to provide learning opportunities girded with tools and strategies that help kids to untangle the complexities, articulate current state, envision desired future state. It's your job to provide tools and strategies (and, yes a bit of wisdom and guidance) that enables these youngsters to identify and embrace the driving forces that will empower them to work through the tough times to a future state that reinforces a spirit of *Can do! Will do!*

The challenges and problems incurred by our young ones will range in difficulty and intensity. The support and resources available will vary. So, you'll need to be dexterous and deft, or better stated, you'll need to provide a learning environment that helps your kids to become dexterous and deft. You can do it . . . you can, you can. Try the bone diagram. It works!

The following example was created by a student in a self-contained classroom for behaviorally challenged kids. He couldn't remember being in any other kind of class, but he wanted out!

Drivers →

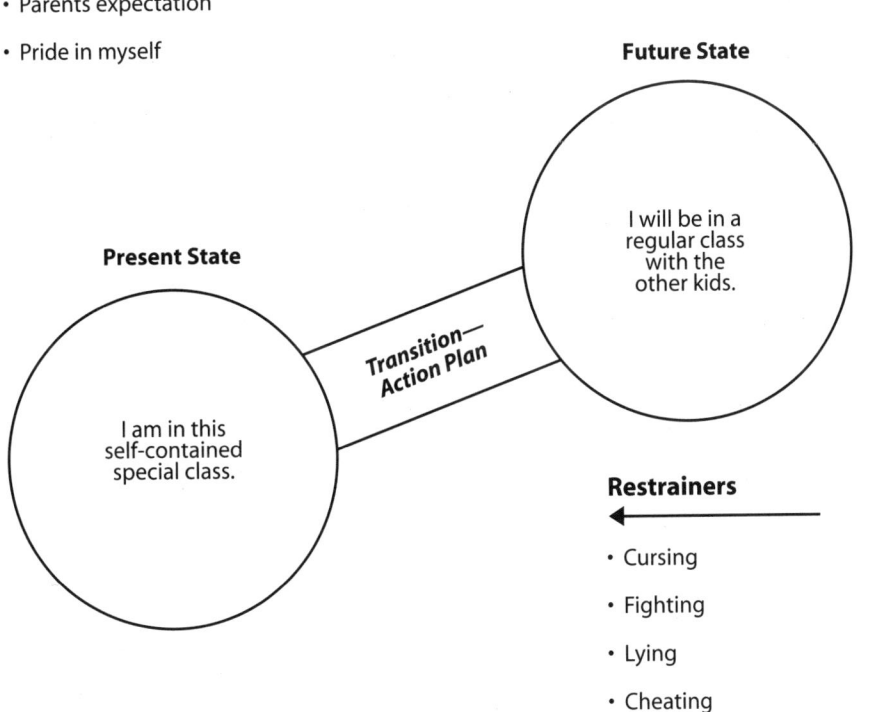

- Parents expectation
- Pride in myself

Present State

I am in this self-contained special class.

Transition—Action Plan

Future State

I will be in a regular class with the other kids.

Restrainers ←

- Cursing
- Fighting
- Lying
- Cheating

An Ah-ha to Remember!

This kid's plan for improvement involved tackling those restrainers one at a time—beginning with data! After tracking the incidence of "cursing" over a couple of weeks, the student could see great improvement! Although at first he concentrated on only one restrainer, he began to see connections. Once he stopped cursing at people so much, his fighting was reduced too! This kid was beginning to feel "in control"!

Chapter Six

CURRICULUM IDEAS FROM A TO Z

LANGUAGE ARTS

- Analyzing writing: A student's paper before and after improvements are made
- Romeo and Juliet before and after Tibalt's death
- Change in a character at the beginning and end of a novel
- Tara before and after the Civil War
- Author's choice of genre based on the audience—the author's actual choice compared to what he might have chosen if there were a different audience

SCIENCE

- Condition of a water supply at two different points in time
- Amount of forest land over time
- Making predictions when conducting experiments—for example, the condition of a substance before and after heating (or cooling, or some other change)
- Identifying present and future properties of an environment

GUIDANCE

- How a team is working together now, and how they would like to work together better in the future
- Present and future state in terms of accomplishing one's goals
- The aging process—how bodies and feelings change over time
- Parent Conferences—clarifying present state and envisioning future state
- Family dynamics and how they can change based on certain events

SOCIAL STUDIES

- The United States before and after the Civil War
- Germany before and after the fall of the Berlin Wall
- Cuba before and after Castro
- Law enforcement procedures before and after "Miranda"

PERFORMING ARTS

- Quality of a musical performance before and after extensive practice
- Silent movies compared to movies with sound

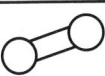

CURRICULUM IDEAS FROM A TO Z

VOCATIONAL EDUCATION

- Auto mechanics: Car engines before and after computerization
- Computer applications: DOS vs. Windows
- Parenting: How parental responsibilities change over time (example for an infant vs. a teenager)
- Keyboarding: A manuscript before and after editing
- Family and Consumer Science: How dietary recommendations have changed over time

HEALTH SCIENCE

- Methods of treating disease at different points in history
- Condition of a heart patient before and after a heart transplant
- A stroke patient's condition before and after the stroke (or before and after physical therapy to help regain function)
- Diabetic before and after insulin treatment

Chapter Six

NOTES

162

NOTES

SUMMARY

A Few Final Words to Help You Get on Your Way . . .

You have the tools, the thought processes, tips for success, key concepts, and lots of examples to help you get on your way. You also have brains in your head and feet in your shoes. And, you know what? Dr. Seuss is absolutely right: *Out there things can happen and frequently do to people as brainy and footsy as you!* So, don't worry, don't stew. You know what you know. You'll decide what to do.

But, let's not get too caught up in the rhyme. We are real people in a real world, and we do recognize that bang-ups and hang-ups can happen. However, you can't get stuck in the waiting place . . . you just can't! Please don't. Try! Learn with your kids through trial and error. These tools work, they really do.

However, even though girded with a host of powerful examples, tips galore, and real-world proof that quality processes work in the classroom, we expect that you still might find yourself wondering, *Do I dare stay out? Do I dare go in? How much can I lose, how much can I win?* And, when you first try using a tool in your real, live classroom with real, live kids, you just might start stewing. Should you turn left or turn right . . . or maybe right-and-three-quarters . . . or, maybe not quite? Should we use this tool or that? Will this work? Will I fall flat on my back?

Congratulations!
Today is your day.
You're off to Great Places!
You're off and away!

You'll be on your way up!
You'll be seeing great sights!
You'll join the high fliers
Who soar to high heights.

Summary

DO YO HAVE THE RIGHT KIND OF KIDS?
Special Feature!

A group of teachers in a workshop watched a video featuring kids in a Total Quality classroom. These teachers were duly impressed. What they saw was awesome. It was clear that the kids were responsible for the learning. They worked in teams, stayed on task, and uncovered the curriculum—with the teacher facilitating the process.

After viewing the video, comments ran rampant with praise, admiration, and high hopes. But, as always happens when using this video clip to demonstrate quality in action, the initial enthusiasm eventually gave way to a wee bit of skepticism, "Those looked like 'high' level kids. I teach 'low' kids" . . . and yada, yada, yada.

Imagine their surprise to learn the demographics of the group:

- all average to low-average in achievement
- a high proportion of economically disadvantaged kids
- several identified as "at risk"

Is there a moral to this story? Of course!

- Don't pigeon-hole.
- Don't assume.
- Don't limit yourself or your kids.

- Do try.
- Do trust the process.
- Do use these tools with any and all grade levels.
- Do use these tools with any and all kinds of kids.

- Just do it!

A Few Final Words to Help You Get on Your Way...

> *Waiting for a train to go*
> *or a bus to come, or a plane to go*
> *or the mail to come, or the rain to go*
> *or the phone to ring, or the snow to snow*
> *or waiting for a Yes or No*
> *or waiting for their hair to grow.*
> *Everyone is just waiting.*
>
> *NO!*
> *That's not for you!*

You might start wondering if you can really take these tools into your classroom to tackle your specific curriculum, with your specific aim, with your specific circumstance. Do you have the right kind of kids? Enough time? The right stuff to do? Too much to do?

All fair questions. But questions with reasonable and well-reasoned answers.

First of all, these tools are not an add-on chore to an already overcrowded curriculum. These tools will help you tackle the curriculum—more efficiently and more effectively. These tools will help your kids take ownership of their learning and boost pride in their workmanship as they work collaboratively with you to cover and uncover your shared curriculum. These tools will help you to actively engage your students as key stakeholders in their learning process. School is so much more meaningful for kids and the work even more worth doing when students actively help to set the goals and plan the tasks to conquer the curriculum. With these tools, learning takes place at a more sophisticated level . . . and the hard work becomes challenging fun as kids learn to problem-solve with real-world skills.

And, no, no, no! These tools are not just for the gifted and talented. These tools can be and are used by teachers with all kinds of kids at all grade levels and in virtually every subject. Look back through the examples and remember: These examples were produced by real, live students with real, live teachers to cover and uncover real-life curriculum while faced with the real-world issues of time, test scores, and available resources. These examples demonstrate that quality tools work in real-life situations, in real for sure classrooms.

And, the results are quite powerful. Using quality tools leads to quality learning—which leads to high performance on high-stakes testing. The data is in: Teachers who use these tools to engage kids in planning, organizing, analyzing, and synthesizing core content of their curriculum would be quick to assure you that improving the process leads to bottom-line results well worth achieving.

Which leads us to just one more thing we want you to think about. These tools do indeed organize and categorize and graphically display complex information. But, that's only the icing on the cake. These tools are not mere graphic organizers, not merely an aggregate of tricks and techniques. So, don't just grab the goodies and go! Ground yourself in the quality principles. Know the purpose and long-term goals of your curriculum, plan the tools into your process, plug them in, then monitor and evaluate the process as you go. Follow this flow and you'll be implementing a strategic learning process—and the tools become quality thinking strategies, quality thinking strategies that really do work!

Okay. We're getting down to doing it . . . and *there's fun to be done!*

There are points to be scored and games to be won. So yes, you're off to great places . . . and, oh, the places you'll go! Will you succeed? Yes! You will indeed! . . . (98 and ³/₄ percent guaranteed.)

Good luck and have fun!

Janet, Jo, and Carolyn

> Don't you just love Dr. Suess?
>
> *We do!*

Summary

THIS REALLY HAPPENED AND COULD HAPPEN TO YOU...
OR COULD IT? YOU KNOW THAT THESE TOOLS WORK FOR ALL OF US!

In a land far, far away . . . just kidding! In a school district much like yours, a group of teachers called the principal of a high-performing school to request a site visit. They specifically asked to visit "low" classes that were using quality tools. The principal carefully sought out those "remedial" and "low level" classes and planned an itinerary for the visitors that he thought would meet their needs and honor their request.

As they toured the designated classes, however, he withheld identifying introductions, simply saying, "This is Miss P's English class," instead of saying, "This is Miss P's remedial English class." And, "This is Mr. B's math class," instead of "This is Mr. B's low-level math class."

After visiting a couple of classes the teachers confronted the principal with a wee bit of anger. "We told you that we wanted to visit low-level classes! We've wasted a trip! All you've showed us are high groups!"

Yep, there's a moral to this story, too! Kids who are currently performing below grade level can improve their performance, their learning skills, and their way of interacting with the curriculum.

Just give them a process, the tools, and a chance!

YOU'LL MOVE MOUNTAINS

On and on you will hike.
And I know you'll hike far
and face up to your problems
whatever they are.

You'll get mixed up, of course,
as you already know.
You'll get mixed up
with many strange birds as you go.

So be sure when you step.
Step with care and great tact
and remember that Life's
a Great Balancing Act.

Just never forget to be dexterous and deft.
And never mix up your right foot with your left.

Dr. Suess
Oh, the Places You'll Go
1990

FOR YOUR INFORMATION...

POWER SOURCES

The following are powerful consulting and training resources—the best of the best!

Covey, Stephen. FranklinCovey Leadership Center. Salt Lake City, UT.

Daggett, Willard. International Center for Leadership in Education. Rexford, NY.

Kagan, Spencer. Kagan Institutes. Riverside, CA.

Langford, David. Langford International. Billings, MT.

Lezotte, Larry. www.effectiveschools.com.

Shipley, Jim. Jim Shipley and Associates. Integrated Systems. Seminole, FL.

Tribus, Myron. mtribus@home.com. Freemont, CA.

Wiggins, Grant. Center for Learning, Assessment and School Structure. Pennington, NJ.

Don't be shy! Tap into these resources!

BIBLIOGRAPHY AND SUGGESTED READINGS

Bloom, B.S. (Ed). *Taxonomy of Educational Objectives: The Classification of Educational Goals. Handbook 1: Cognitive Domain.* New York: McKay. 1956.

Byrnes, Margaret A., and Cornesky, Robert A. *Quality Fusion.* Orange, FL: Cornesky & Associates, Inc. 1994.

Covey, Stephen. *The Seven Habits of Highly Effective People.* Thorndike, ME: G. K. Hall. 1997. ©1989.

Deming, W. Edwards. *Out of the Crisis.* Cambridge, MA: MIT Center for Advanced Engineering Study. 1986.

Glasser, William. *The Quality School.* New York: Harper Perennial. 1992.

Kagan, Spencer. *Cooperative Learning Resources for Teachers.* Riverside, CA: Resources for Teachers. 1989.

Langford, David P., and Cleary, Barbara A., Ph.D. *Orchestrating Learning with Quality.* Milwaukee, WI: Quality Press. 1995.

Lezotte, Larry. Dr. Lezotte offers many resources on his website: www.effectiveschools.com.

For Your Information

McClanahan, Elaine, and Wicks, Carolyn. *Future Force—Kids That Want To, Can, and Do!* Chino Hills, CA: PACT Publishing. 1993.

Schargel, Franklin P. *Transforming Education Through Total Quality Management.* Princeton Junction, NJ: Eye on Education. 1994.

Seuss, Dr. *Oh, The Places You'll Go!* New York: Random House. 1990.

Tribus, Myron. Dr. Tribus provides 20+ articles which are free and accessible to all. For his reports go to:

http://deming.ces.clemson.edu/pub/den/deming_tribus.htm

For more information on Dr. Tribus' work with Reuven Feuerstein:

http://www.icelp.org

Wiggins, Grant, and McTighe, Jay. *Understanding by Design.* Upper Saddle River, NJ: Merrill/Prentice Hall. 2001.

For Your Information

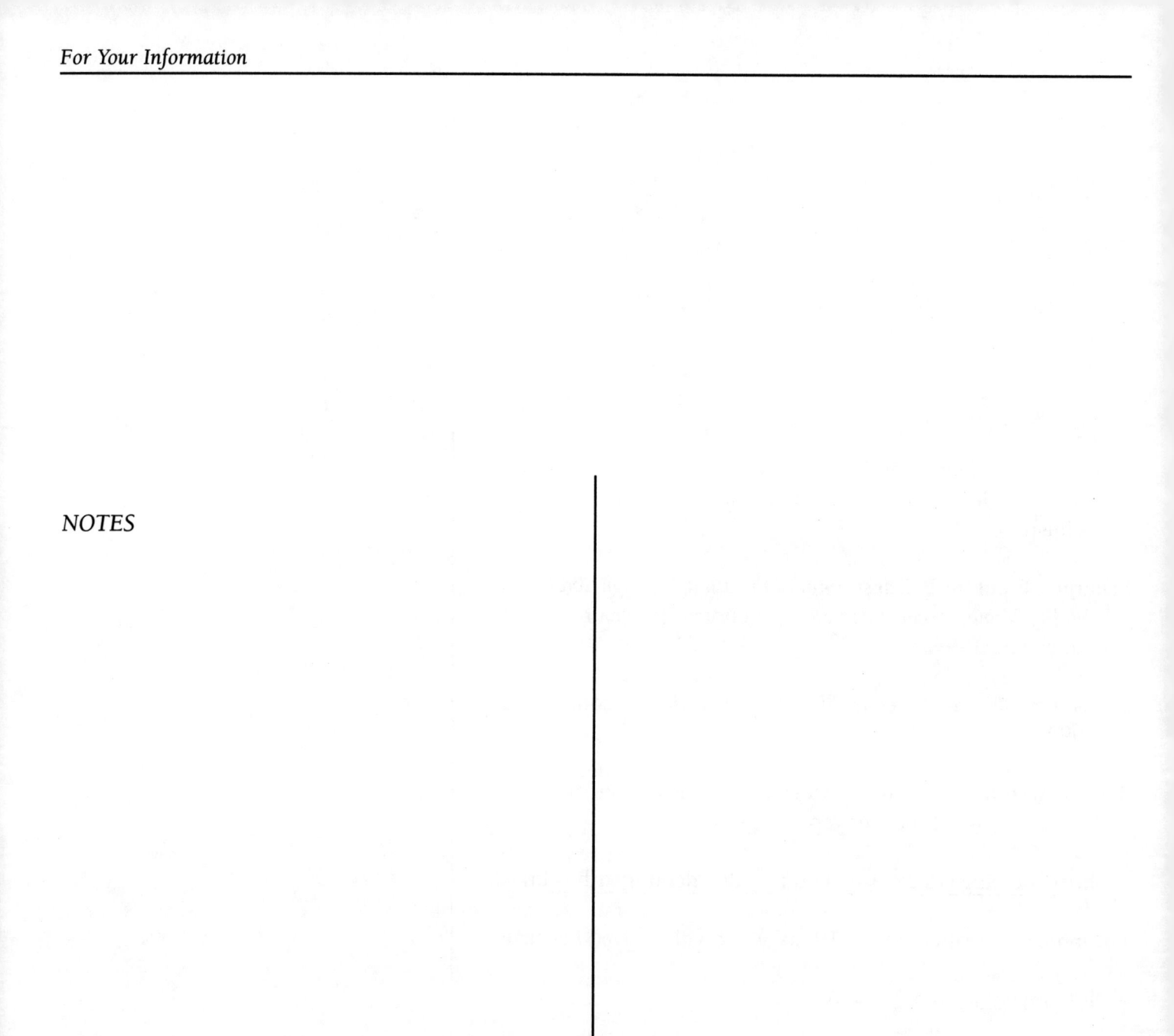

NOTES

NOTES

For Your Information

NOTES

NOTES

For Your Information

QUALITY TOOLS PULL-OUT PAGES

Note: The following pull-out pages are provided for you to copy, enlarge, pass out to your kids, and for any purpose that helps you take these tools into your classroom.

Be creative! Enjoy! Do it!

TOOLS

What?	What Does It Look Like?	What Is This Used For?	Where Can I Find It?
Fishbone Diagram		To analyze cause and effect or to organize information.	Ch. 1, pp. 17-39
Lotus Diagram		Organize information.	Ch. 2, pp. 43-63
Affinity Diagram		Generate (brainstorm) information and categorize by likeness.	Ch. 3, pp. 67-85
Force Field Analysis		Analyze drivers and restrainers.	Ch. 4, pp. 89-109
Flowchart		Define a process.	Ch. 5, pp. 113-133
Bone Diagram		Analyze transition from present to future state.	Ch. 6, pp. 137-161

Fishbone Diagram

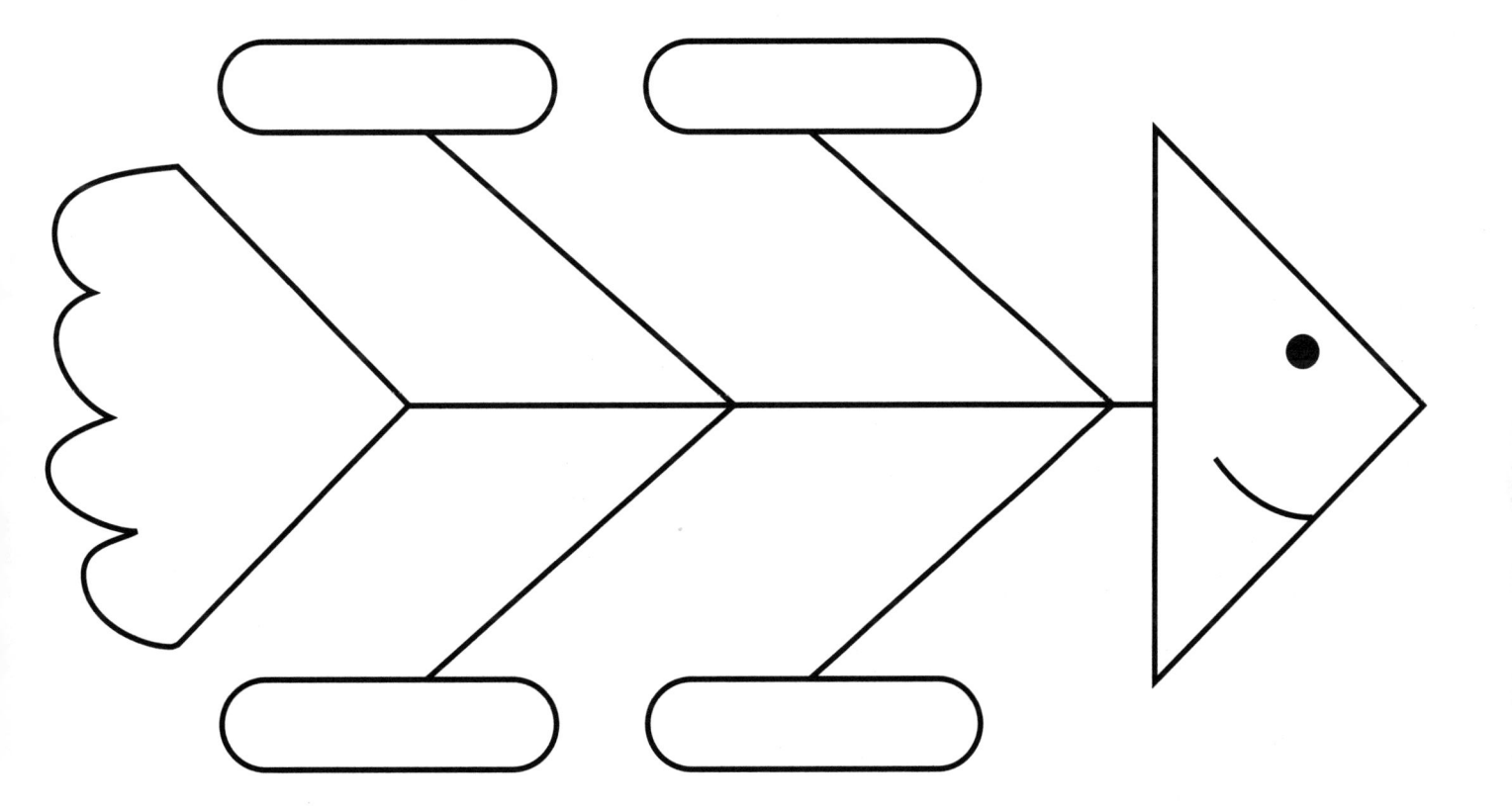

Fishbone Diagram

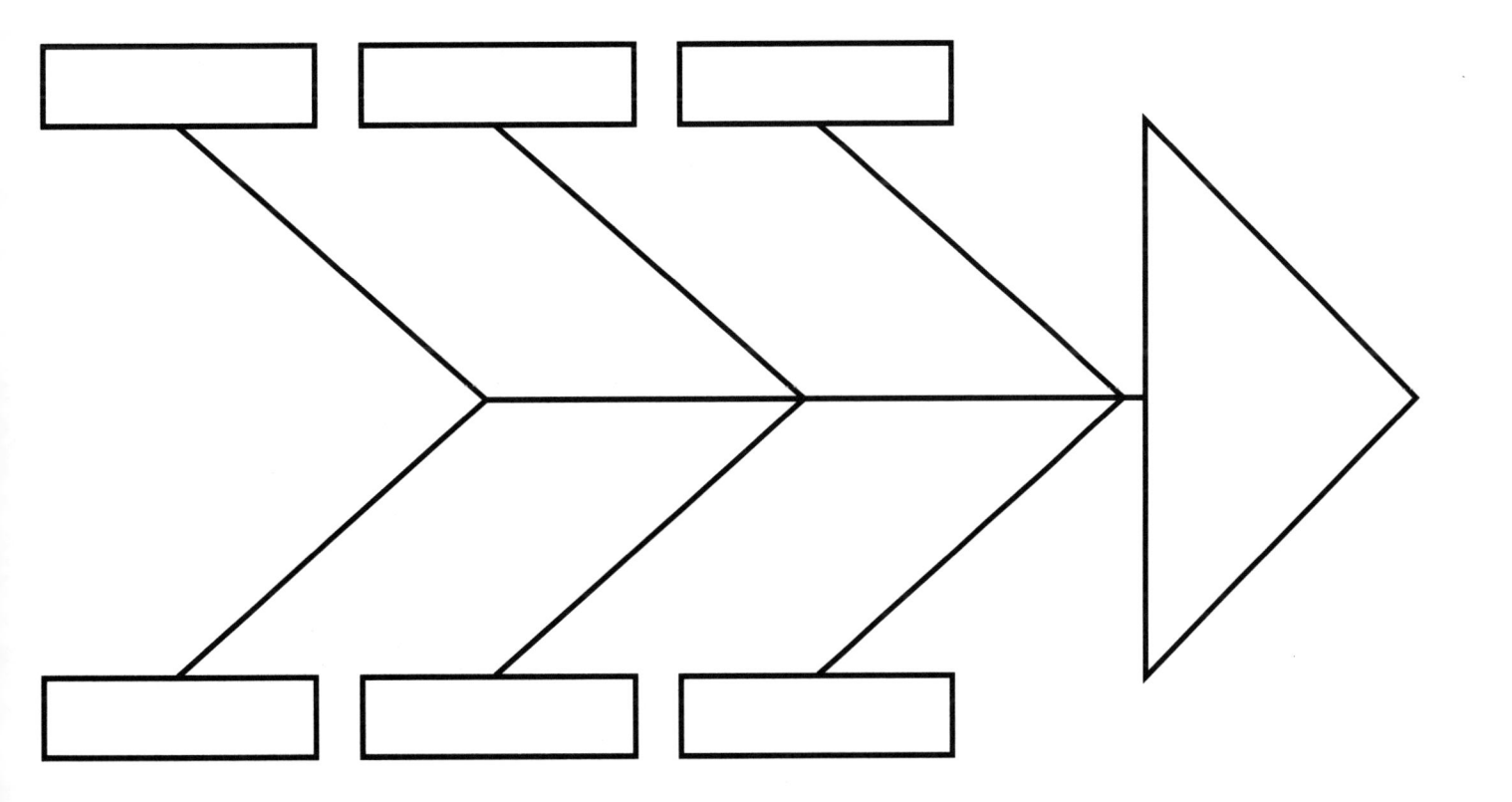

Lotus Diagram

Lotus Diagram

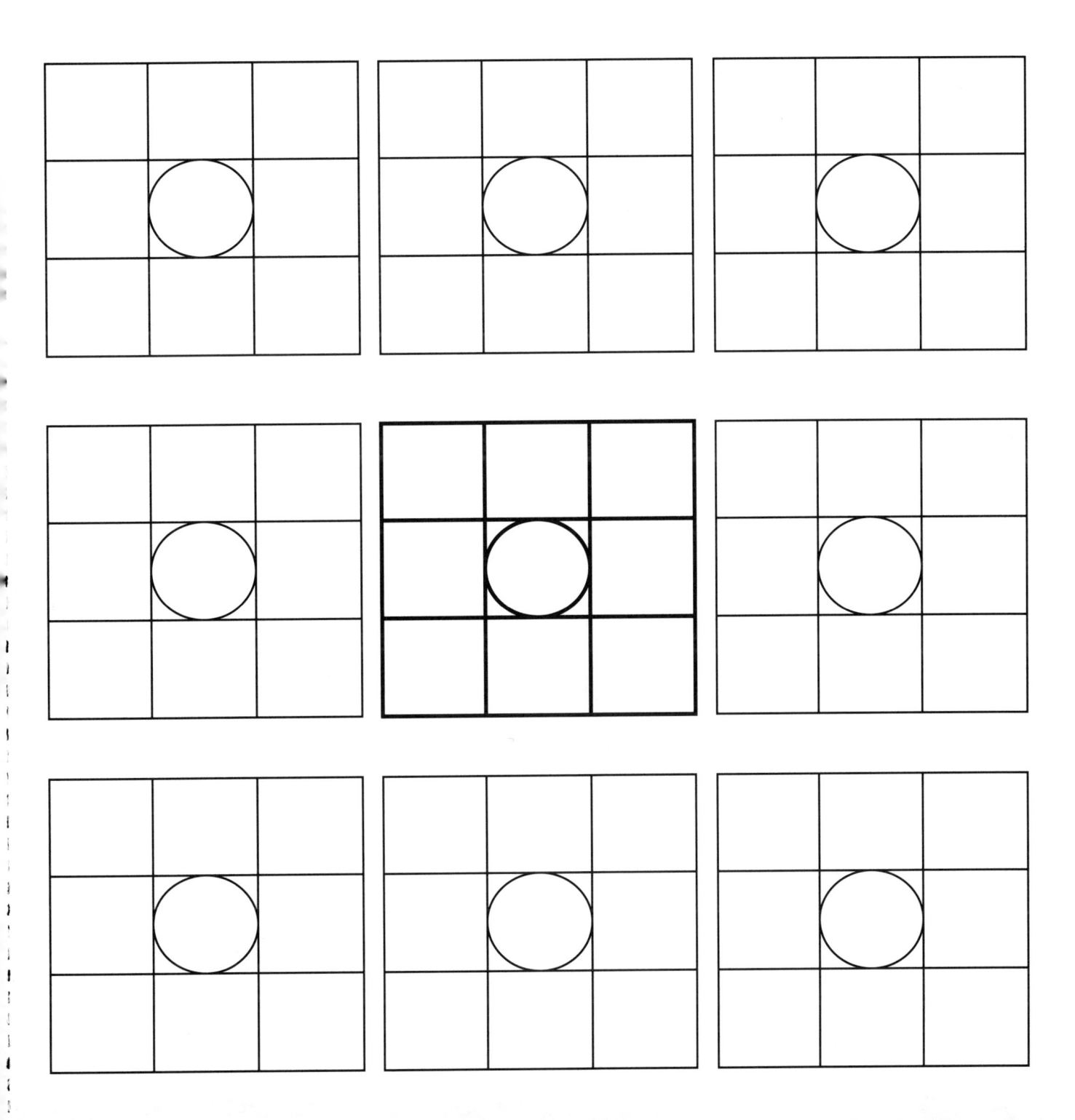

Force Field Analysis

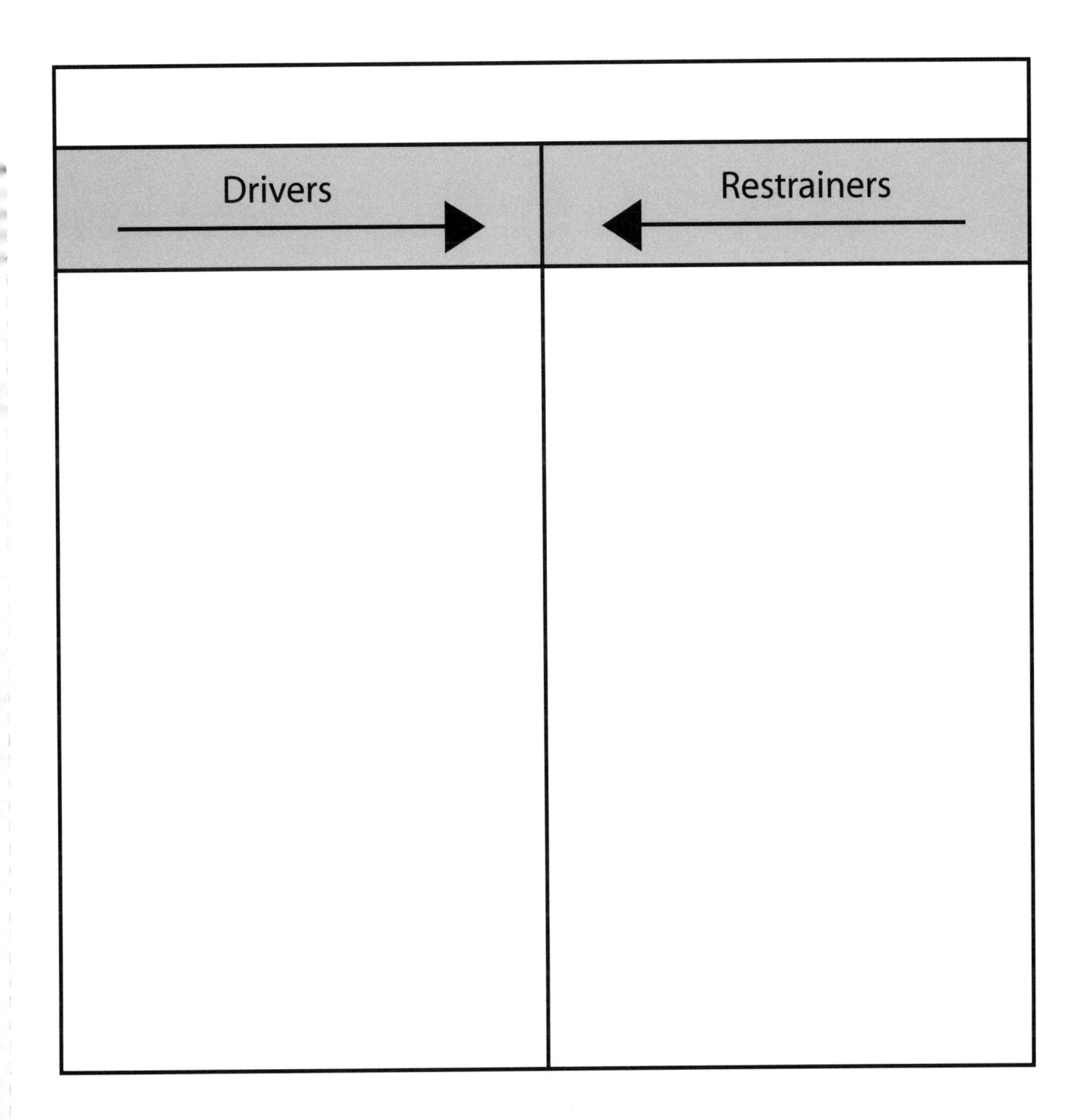

Drivers →	← Restrainers

Flowchart Symbols

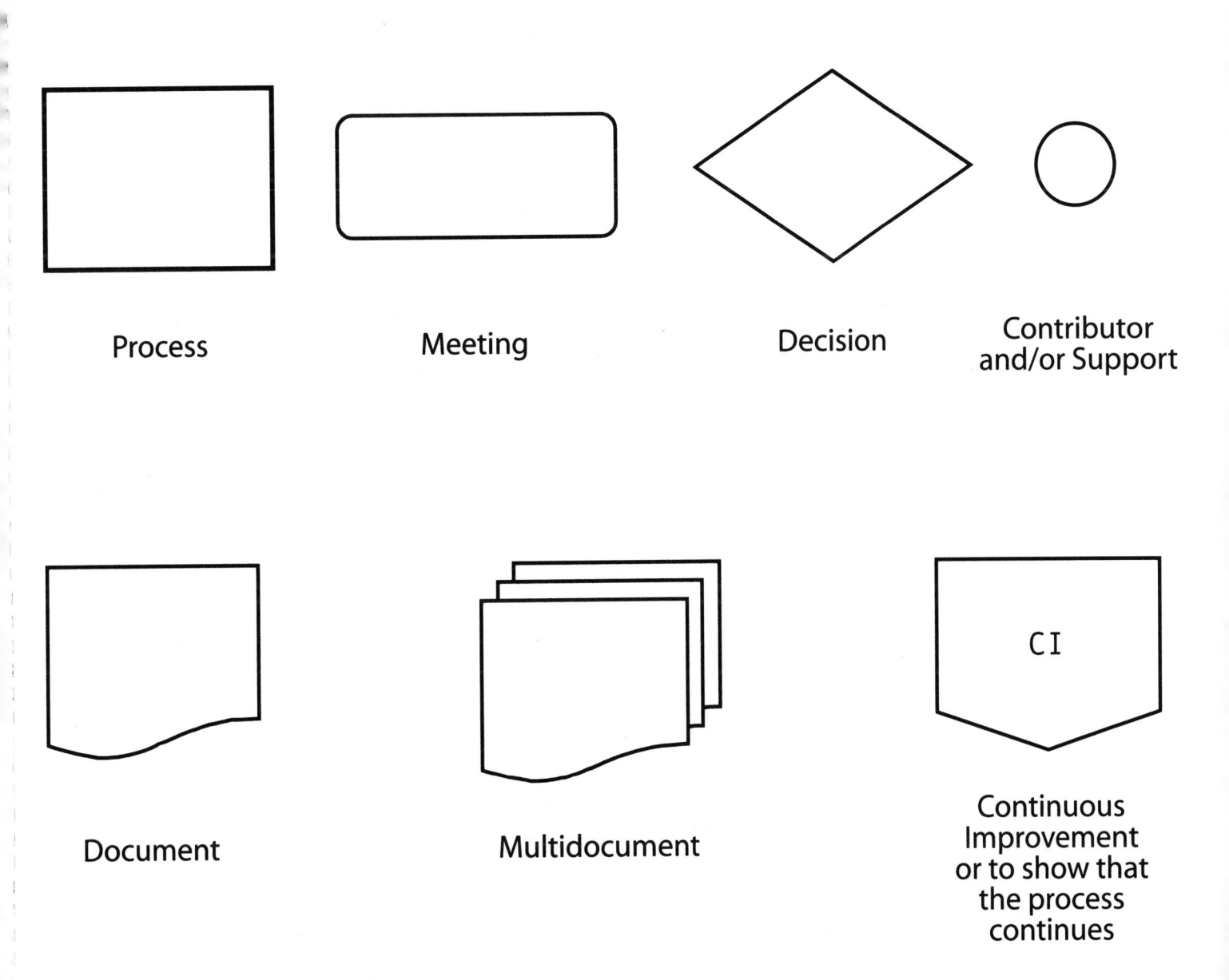

Process	Meeting	Decision	Contributor and/or Support

Document	Multidocument	Continuous Improvement or to show that the process continues

CI

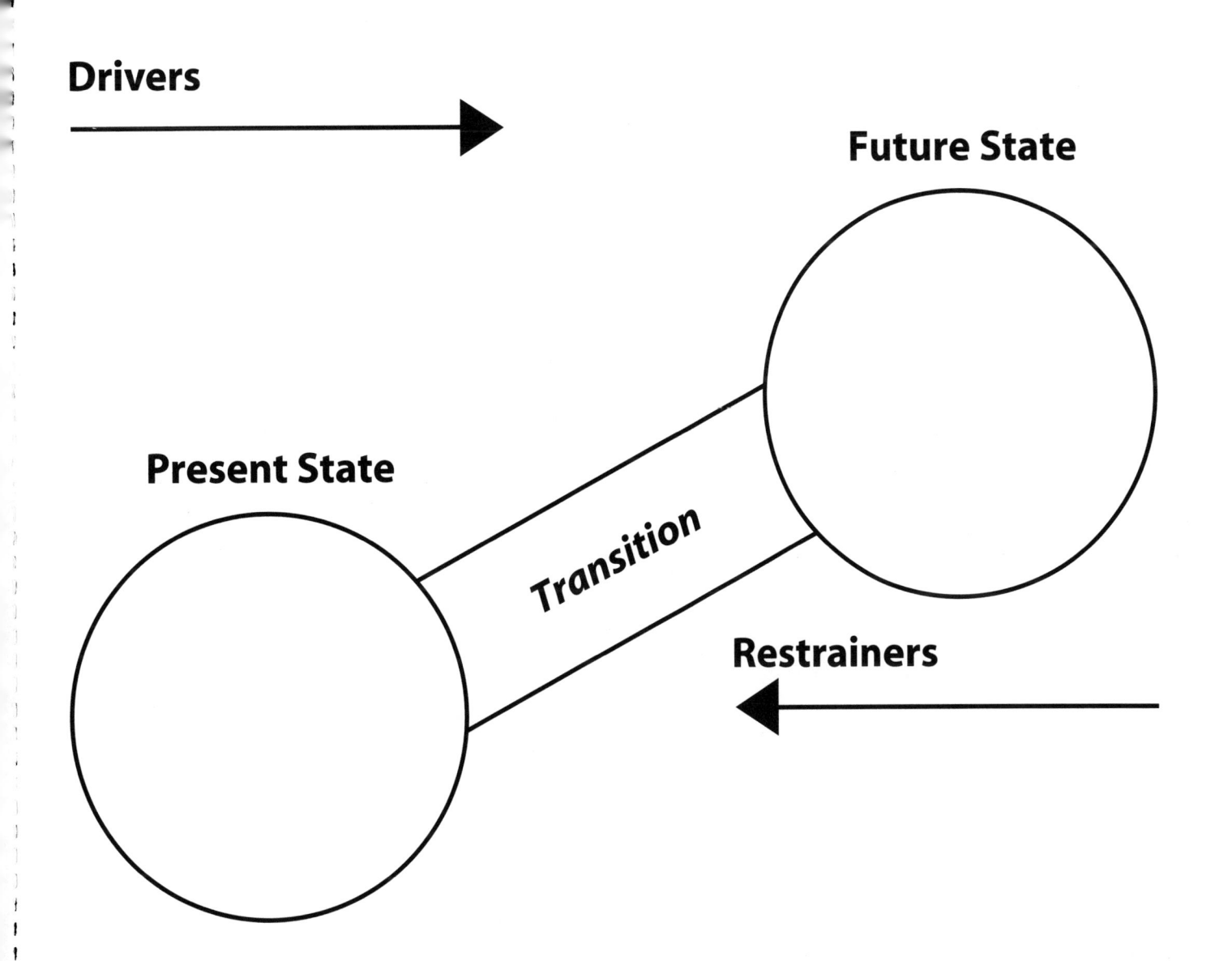

Bone Diagram

Drivers

Future State

Present State

Transition

Restrainers

For additional copies please complete the order form below,
or call our toll free number for more information.

Plugged In! Using Quality Tools to Conquer the Curriculum by Carolyn Wicks, Janet Peregoy, and Jo Wheeler is a user-friendly and dynamic resource designed specifically for those of you who are in the trenches, for those of you who understand and confront the everyday rigors of the overcrowded and ever-changing curriculum, high-stakes testing, and the need for real-world problem solving.

Plugged In! is a resource you'll want to take with you on your quality journey . . . regardless of whether you're just starting out or moving right along!

(Please Print)

Name _____

Address _____

City _____ State _____ Zip _____

Phone (_____) _____

Send order to:

ClassAction
Coast to Coast Connection
P.O. Box 3040
New Bern, NC 28564-3040

Or call to order:

1-800-705-6176
1-866-358-4314 fax
1-252-636-0193
1-252-636-3865 fax

Price	**Quantity**	**Amount**
$24.95		
	Subtotal	
	Delivery in NC Add 6.5% Sales Tax	
Shipping & Handling $4.00 for one book—10% on orders of 2 or more		
	Total	

Bulk Orders

Please call for discounts on pricing, shipping, and handling.

For additional copies please complete the order form below,
or call our toll free number for more information.

Plugged In! Using Quality Tools to Conquer the Curriculum by Carolyn Wicks, Janet Peregoy, and Jo Wheeler is a user-friendly and dynamic resource designed specifically for those of you who are in the trenches, for those of you who understand and confront the everyday rigors of the overcrowded and ever-changing curriculum, high-stakes testing, and the need for real-world problem solving.

Plugged In! is a resource you'll want to take with you on your quality journey . . . regardless of whether you're just starting out or moving right along!

(Please Print)

Name _____

Address _____

City _____ State _____ Zip _____

Phone (_____) _____

Send order to:

ClassAction
Coast to Coast Connection
P.O. Box 3040
New Bern, NC 28564-3040

Or call to order:

1-800-705-6176
1-866-358-4314 fax
1-252-636-0193
1-252-636-3865 fax

Price	Quantity	Amount
$24.95		
	Subtotal	
	Delivery in NC Add 6.5% Sales Tax	
	Shipping & Handling $4.00 for one book—10% on orders of 2 or more	
	Total	

Bulk Orders
Please call for discounts on pricing, shipping, and handling.

For additional copies please complete the order form below,
or call our toll free number for more information.

Plugged In! Using Quality Tools to Conquer the Curriculum by Carolyn Wicks, Janet Peregoy, and Jo Wheeler is a user-friendly and dynamic resource designed specifically for those of you who are in the trenches, for those of you who understand and confront the everyday rigors of the overcrowded and ever-changing curriculum, high-stakes testing, and the need for real-world problem solving.

Plugged In! is a resource you'll want to take with you on your quality journey . . . regardless of whether you're just starting out or moving right along!

(Please Print)

Name _____

Address _____

City _____ State _____ Zip _____

Phone (_____) _____

Send order to:

ClassAction
Coast to Coast Connection
P.O. Box 3040
New Bern, NC 28564-3040

Or call to order:

1-800-705-6176
1-866-358-4314 fax
1-252-636-0193
1-252-636-3865 fax

Price	Quantity	Amount
$24.95		
Subtotal		
Delivery in NC Add 6.5% Sales Tax		
Shipping & Handling $4.00 for one book—10% on orders of 2 or more		
Total		

Bulk Orders
Please call for discounts on pricing, shipping, and handling.